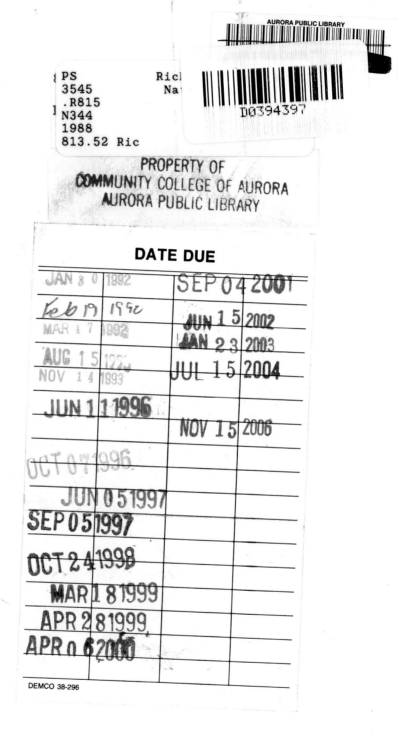

DATE DUE

JAN 3 0 1992	SEP 0 4 2001
Feb 19 1992	JUN 1 5 2002
MAR 1 7 1992	JAN 2 3 2003
AUG 1 5 199?	JUL 1 5 2004
NOV 1 4 1993	
JUN 1 1 1996	
	NOV 1 5 2006
OCT 0 7 1996	
JUN 0 5 1997	
SEP 0 5 1997	
OCT 2 4 1998	
MAR 1 8 1999	
APR 2 8 1999	
APR 0 6 2000	

DEMCO 38-296

Modern Critical Interpretations

Richard Wright's
Native Son

Modern Critical Interpretations

These and other titles in preparation

Modern Critical Interpretations

Richard Wright's
Native Son

Edited and with an introduction by

Harold Bloom
Sterling Professor of the Humanities
Yale University

Chelsea House Publishers
NEW YORK ◊ PHILADELPHIA

© 1988 by Chelsea House Publishers, a division
of Main Line Book Co.

Introduction © 1987 by Harold Bloom

Printed and bound in the United States of America

10   9   8   7   6   5   4   3   2

∞ The paper used in this publication meets the minimum
requirements of the American National Standard for Permanence
of Paper for Printed Library Materials, Z39.48–1984.

Library of Congress Cataloging-in-Publication Data
Richard Wright's Native son / edited and with an introduction
 by Harold Bloom.
     p. cm.—(Modern critical interpretations)
  Bibliography: p.
  Includes index.
  Summary: A collection of critical essays on Wright's novel,
arranged chronologically in the order of their original
publication.
  ISBN 1-55546-055-0
  1. Wright, Richard, 1908–1960. Native son. [1. Wright,
Richard, 1908–1960. Native son. 2. American literature—History
and criticism.] I. Series.
PS3545.R815N344   1988
813'.52—dc19   87–30402
                                                            CIP
                                                            AC

APR   1990

Contents

Editor's Note

This book gathers together a representative selection of the best critical interpretations of Richard Wright's novel *Native Son*. The critical essays are reprinted here in the chronological order of their original publication. I am greatly indebted to Henry Finder for his erudite aid in editing this volume.

My introduction centers upon the aesthetic limitations of *Native Son*, while acknowledging Richard Wright's heroic stance as one of the founders of black literature in the United States of America. Dan McCall begins the chronological sequence of criticism with a distinction between Frantz Fanon's view of Bigger, which is that murder is his only social reality, and McCall's own judgment, which is that Bigger's violences "are at the mercy of the system which engendered them."

In Roger Rosenblatt's reading, Bigger is "a man who has discovered the full meaning of the kingdom of hell," while Joel Roache's analysis of Wright's essay on his novel's genesis concludes that *Native Son* was an attempt "to return art to its place as an expression of real social forces."

Michael G. Cooke sees Wright as a novelist who "sets forth without mercy the state, and the cause, of self-cancellation," which is a more dialectical view than that of Joyce Anne Joyce, for whom Bigger is a tragic hero, comparable to the great protagonists of the tradition of Western tragedy. Her interpretation is in turn very different from the exegesis of Louis Tremaine, whose Bigger is a ruined sensibility, which clings "with a kind of desperate joy to the fear and hate that have destroyed" its life.

Valerie Smith discovers in Bigger an image of alienation that yet has a capacity for creative self-understanding. In the most sophisticated critical treatment of *Native Son*, Barbara Johnson reveals in the novel an implied figure of the black woman as the *reader* of Wright's work.

Joseph T. Skerrett, Jr., centers upon the making of *Native Son,* a work exposing "the essential loneliness incumbent on a person who, for whatever reason, must create a sense of values for himself." In this volume's final essay, David Bradley, author of *South Street,* recounts his first and successive readings of *Native Son,* reminding us that it was a first novel and that it remains a testimony to what were once our social realities.

Introduction

What remains of Richard Wright's work if we apply to it only aesthetic standards of judgment? This is to assume that strictly aesthetic standards exist, and that we know what they are. Wright, in *Native Son,* essentially the son of Theodore Dreiser, could not rise always even to Dreiser's customarily bad level of writing. Here is Bigger Thomas, condemned to execution, at the start of his death vigil:

> In self-defense he shut out the night and day from his mind, for if he had thought of the sun's rising and setting, of the moon or the stars, of clouds or rain, he would have died a thousand deaths before they took him to the chair. To accustom his mind to death as much as possible, he made all the world beyond his cell a vast gray land where neither night nor day was, peopled by strange men and women whom he could not understand, but with those lives he longed to mingle once before he went.
>
> He did not eat now; he simply forced food down his throat without tasting it, to keep the gnawing pain of hunger away, to keep from feeling dizzy. And he did not sleep; at intervals he closed his eyes for a while, no matter what the hour, then opened them at some later time to resume his brooding. He wanted to be free of everything that stood between him and his end, him and the full and terrible realization that life was over without meaning, without anything being settled, without conflicting impulses being resolved.

If we isolate these paragraphs, then we do not know the color or background of the man awaiting execution. The intense sociological pathos of Wright's narrative vanishes, and we are left in the first paragraph with an inadequate rhetoric: "shut out the night and day," "died a thousand deaths," "a vast gray land," "strange men and women," "with those lives he longed to mingle." Yet the second paragraph is even more unsatisfactory, as the exact word is nowhere: "gnawing pain of hunger," "resume his brooding," "full and terrible realization," "conflicting impulses being resolved." Wright's narrative requires from him at this point some mode of language that would individuate Bigger's dread, that would catch and fix the ordeal of a particular black man condemned by a white society. Unfortunately, Wright's diction does not allow us even to distinguish Bigger's horror from any other person's apprehension of judicial murder. Nor does Bigger's own perspective enter into Wright's rhetorical stance. The problem is not so much Wright's heritage from Dreiser's reductive naturalism as it is, plainly stated, a bad authorial ear.

It is rather too late to make so apparently irrelevant an observation, since Wright has become a canonical author, for wholesome societal purposes with which I am happy to concur. Rereading *Native Son* or *Black Boy* cannot be other than an overdetermined activity, since Wright is a universally acknowledged starting point for black literature in contemporary America. Canonical critics of Wright speak of him as a pioneer, a man of rare courage, as a teacher and forerunner. None of this can or should be denied. I myself would praise him for will, force, and drive, human attributes that he carried just over the border of aesthetic achievement, without alas getting very far once he had crossed over. His importance transcends the concerns of a strictly literary criticism, and reminds the critic of the claims of history, society, political economy, and the longer records of oppression and injustice that history continues to scant.

II

Bigger Thomas can be said to have become a myth without first having been a convincing representation of human character and personality. Wright listed five "Biggers" he had encountered in actuality, five violent youths called "bad Niggers" by the whites. The most impressive, Bigger No. 5, was a knife-wielding, prideful figure "who always rode the Jim Crow streetcars without paying and sat wherever he pleased." For this group of precursors of his own protagonist in *Native Son*, Wright gave us a moving valediction:

> The Bigger Thomases were the only Negroes I know of
> who consistently violated the Jim Crow laws of the South
> and got away with it, at least for a sweet brief spell.
> Eventually, the whites who restricted their lives made them
> pay a terrible price. They were shot, hanged, maimed,
> lynched, and generally hounded until they were either dead
> or their spirits broken.

Wright concluded this same introduction to *Native Son* with his own
vision of the United States as of March 7, 1940:

> I feel that I'm lucky to be alive to write novels today, when
> the whole world is caught in the pangs of war and change.
> Early American writers, Henry James and Nathaniel Haw-
> thorne, complained bitterly about the bleakness and flatness
> of the American scene. But I think that if they were alive,
> they'd feel at home in modern America. True, we have no
> great church in America; our national traditions are still of
> such a sort that we are not wont to brag of them: and we
> have no army that's above the level of mercenary fighters;
> we have no group acceptable to the whole of our country
> upholding certain humane values; we have no rich symbols,
> no colorful rituals. We have only a money-grubbing,
> industrial civilization. But we do have in the Negro the
> embodiment of a past tragic enough to appease the spiritual
> hunger of even a James; and we have in the oppression of
> the Negro a shadow athwart our national life dense and
> heavy enough to satisfy even the gloomy broodings of a
> Hawthorne. And if Poe were alive, he would not have to
> invent horror; horror would invent him.

The citation of James, Hawthorne, and Poe is gratuitous, and the
perspective upon the United States in the months preceding the fall of
France lacks authority and precision, even in its diction. But the dense
and heavy shadow athwart our national life indubitably was there,
always had been there, and for many is there still. That shadow is
Richard Wright's mythology, and his embryonic strength. He was not
found by Henry James, or by Hawthorne, or by Poe, and scarcely
would have benefited by such a finding. A legitimate son of Theodore
Dreiser, he nevertheless failed to write in *Native Son* a *Sister Carrie* or
a new version of *An American Tragedy*. The reality of being a gifted

young black in the United States of the thirties and forties proved too oppressive for the limited purposes of a narrative fiction. Rereading *Native Son* is an experience of renewing the dialectical awareness of history and society, but is not in itself an aesthetic experience.

And yet, I do not think that *Native Son* and its reception present us with a merely aesthetic dilemma. In the afterword to the current paperback reprint of *Native Son*, one of Wright's followers, John Reilly, defends Bigger Thomas by asserting that "the description of Mary's murder makes clear that the white world is the cause of the violent desires and reactions" that led Bigger to smother poor Mary. I would think that what the description makes clear enough is that Bigger is indeed somewhat overdetermined, but to ascribe the violence of his desires and reactions to any context whatsoever is to reduce him to the status of a replicant or of a psychopathic child. The critical defenders of *Native Son* must choose. Either Bigger Thomas is a responsible consciousness, and so profoundly culpable, or else only the white world is responsible and culpable, which means, however, that Bigger ceases to be of fictive interest and becomes an ideogram rather than a persuasive representation of a possible human being. Wright, coming tragically early in what was only later to become his own tradition, was not able to choose and so left us with something between an ideological image and the mimesis of an actuality.

The Bad Nigger

Dan McCall

In his essay on Bigger's birth, Wright said that "life had made the plot over and over again, to the extent that I knew it by heart." Repeatedly he had seen black boys picked off the streets to be charged with an unsolved case of "rape." "This thing happens so often that to my mind it had become a representative symbol of the Negro's uncertain position in America." Robert Nixon was apprehended and sent sprawling across the front page of the *Tribune* while Wright was in mid-passage with Bigger Thomas. The actual case is a part of history—as the novel is part of the literary history—of the thing itself. In Chicago in 1938 two black men were testifying to the myth, one with a brick and the other with a book.

Richard, like Bigger, lived in a Chicago slum with his mother. As an insurance agent Wright had visited various black kitchenettes like the one with which his book would begin. In the opening scene the people driven so closely together are driven violently apart. Wright would say the following year, in *Twelve Million Black Voices,* "The kitchenette throws desperate and unhappy people into an unbearable closeness of association, thereby increasing latent friction, giving birth to never-ending quarrels of recrimination, accusation, and vindictiveness, producing warped personalities." The full recognition of how the "kitchenette" (which refers to the cramped apartment itself, not just the cooking area) forms Bigger's sensibility—or how it deprived him of what we would call a "sensibility"—was one of Wright's most daring and significant choices.

From *The Example of Richard Wright.* © 1969 by Dan McCall. Harcourt Brace & World, 1969.

In "Many Thousands Gone," Baldwin saw that "Bigger has no discernible relationship to himself, to his own life, to his own people, nor to any other people" and because of that "a necessary dimension has been cut away." But that was surely Wright's point; he knew that he was cutting away a dimension. He said in "How 'Bigger' Was Born" that he planned for his black boy to be "estranged from the religion and the folk culture of his race"—a statement that shows that Wright was consciously pulling things away and not, as the criticism against Wright might lead one to believe, that Wright just didn't know how to show them. In *Twelve Million Black Voices* he summarized:

> Perhaps never in history has a more utterly unprepared folk wanted to go to the city; we were barely born as a folk when we headed for the tall and sprawling centers of steel and stone. We, who were landless on the land; we, who had barely managed to live in family groups; we, who needed the ritual and guidance of institutions to hold our atomized lives together in lines of purpose; we, who had known only relationships to people and not relationships to things; we, who had never belonged to any organizations except the church and burial societies; we, who had had our personalities blasted with two hundred years of slavery and had been turned loose to shift for ourselves.

In the figure of Bigger Thomas, Wright was trying to show the ultimate sense of horror: unpreparedness set loose in a metropolis. Bigger has nothing to hold him back and nothing to define his responses other than the blackness of his skin. He is, as his mother wails, "black crazy"; his mind is crazed by his color. He is incapable of a nonracial thought. His obsession produces what Wright would later call "The State of Exaggeration." In *White Man, Listen!* Wright says that "one of the aspects of life of the American Negro that has amazed observers is the emotional intensity with which he attacks ordinary, daily problems." How can the mind ever relax or grow when its defining problem is always and unbearably one thing? Wright offers as an example the problem a Negro has in renting a place to live; the overriding question, the one that gathers all the usual questions of whether the place is clean, whether it is well-made, whether it's near a school, whether it's near stores, is only one question: can a black person live there? And as the great migration moved northward in the twenties and thirties the black folk found their answer. They would live in the kitchenette.

This "state of exaggeration" that Wright speaks of is most clearly seen in the kitchenette by an overwhelming fear of being looked at. The kitchenette means lack of privacy. On the first page of *Native Son,* when people get out of bed, the first words are "Turn your heads so I can dress." Day after day in the ghetto that is the call to society; and on the second day of Wright's story, in the center section of his book, Vera repeats the line "Turn your head so I can dress." Even when one is dressed, the fear continues at the breakfast table, this horror of being seen.

> "Stop looking at me, Bigger!"
> "Aw, shut up and eat your breakfast!"
> "Ma, make 'im stop looking at me!"
> "I ain't looking at her, Ma!"
> "You *is!*" Vera said.

And so it goes, on into the night where children are given their sexual education because the mother and father cannot not give it to them. After his murders Bigger roams the ghetto apartment houses, climbing them and peering into windows where he sees

> through a window without shades . . . a room in which were two small iron beds with sheets dirty and crumpled. In one bed sat three naked black children looking across the room to the other bed on which lay a man and woman, both naked and black. . . . There were quick, jerky movements on the bed where the man and woman lay, and the three children were watching.

Biggers sees it as a memory, for he, too, had often "awakened and watched his father and mother." He climbs on up with one last look in at "the man and woman moving jerkily in tight embrace, and the three children watching."

Wright's point is not to deny the Negro's "folk culture." He was trying to show that for those urban slum dwellers the folk culture was swallowed in unbearable closeness. This emptiness and fear of being looked at Bigger carries with him all the day long. The scene which begins the book is present at the very center of the crime where Bigger is hysterical at not being able to get the full human form into a tight place. He has to cut off the head. Bigger's head, his sensibility, was cut off in the kitchenette. (And the severed head appears in his dream as his own.) At the end of the book Max keeps asking Bigger what Mary Dalton had done to him that made Bigger say, "I ain't sorry she's dead." Bigger struggles for the answer; all he knows is that he hated her. He stammers and tries to find it and then vaguely he gets an image of his sister

> Vera, sitting on the edge of a chair crying because he had shamed her by "looking" at her; he saw her rise and fling her shoe at him. He shook his head confused.

That is it: racial misery is indecent exposure.

And so Wright would tell us at the beginning of his story that Bigger's relationship to his family was that "he lived with them, but behind a wall, a curtain." When he relates to black people he takes his violence out on them. His hate bottles up and has to get out; since it cannot reach its stimulus, the white man, it is expelled on blacks. He corners his pal, Gus, and holds a knife blade at his mouth, saying, "Lick it." What he wants to do, of course, is hold it at the white man's lips, draw blood from the white man's tongue. But he can't get at him. Bigger "had heard it said that white people felt it was good when one Negro killed another; it meant that they had one Negro less to contend with." When a Negro says he is afraid to go to Mississippi because "down there they'd as soon kill you as look at you" he does not refer merely to the white race. Bigger cannot feel "guilt" about his murders. His is a mind in which "guilt" plays as negligible a part as it did in the whites who set fire to Bobo. Bigger cannot say, "I have killed a *human being,*" for there are no human beings on his planet. Bessie was not at all his "sweetheart," only the "girl" he had because other boys had them. His relationship to her is his relationship to the black community; he will use and enjoy her when he can and strike out when she gets in his way. "The black girl was merely 'evidence.' And under it all he knew that the white people did not really care about Bessie's being killed."

Bigger is, then, one of the Negro's "roles" (in spite of the continuing objection that he is not) and the white reader can see it more clearly now as black voices from the ghetto begin to come out with verification of how accurate Bigger was. Anyone who has read *The Autobiography of Malcolm X* or *Manchild in the Promised Land* or Eldridge Cleaver's remarkable *Soul on Ice* can see Biggers in the characters the authors draw around them and explore, with considerable courage, in themselves. Wright does not, as Baldwin said, "cut a necessary dimension away." Again, white America beat him to it. Had Wright not portrayed Bigger in this way he would have been cutting a "necessary dimension away" not from his figure but from the importance of the forces that would make him what he was. To create a "folk tradition" in the slum—that is, to create whole human beings in a brutally fragmented world—would not be to take that world seriously. It would be a gross underestimation of how massive the damage is. Wright saw that if people do not have any chance to get culture it is rather unlikely that they will have its blessings.

When Bigger goes out onto the street he sees a poster for Buckley's campaign: "IF YOU BREAK THE LAW, YOU CAN'T WIN!" And, as Bigger knows, if you don't break it, you keep losing. This is the white man's law. What Bigger has available to him is no "folk tradition" but the glittery expression of the white civilization. He goes to a movie, *The Gay Woman,* in which he gets that tradition in "scenes of cocktail drinking, dancing, golfing, swimming, and spinning roulette wheels, a rich young white woman kept clandestine appointments with her lover while her millionaire husband was busy in the offices of a vast paper mill." If Bigger went to that world of money and fancy sex, the white folks would run—thinking, as Bigger's chum says, "a gorilla broke loose from the zoo and put on a tuxedo."

When Bigger actually goes into the white mansion where "the gay woman" lives, he goes as a chauffeur. His position behind the wheel is a gross parody of his deepest wish: to be behind the stick of the airplane. Passionate to get out of his prison, to roam the skies, he is only a "driver." Bigger is constantly assuming such poses that are emblematic stances of the Negro. When he puts the white maiden in the trunk and carries her down to the furnace he is frozen for a moment as the jolly redcap at the station. The black destroyer is a porter. Climbing buildings he is the giant darky we blew up onto the screen, the "Bigger" black man; he stands roaring on the rooftops until white technology sends him plummeting to the street below. And *King Kong* ends with the assertion that "beauty killed the beast" just as *Native Son* shows how the beast—if given a chance—will kill the beauty.

The scene with Jan and Mary is one of gross comedy. In order to make Bigger feel at home Jan says first of all in the restaurant, "You like fried chicken?" (And decades later Lenny Bruce would begin his sketch, "How to Make a Negro Feel Comfortable at a Party" with the white host going over to the black guest—"Can I get you something? Piece of watermelon? Chicken leg?") Jan and Mary are locked almost as tightly in stereotypes as is Bigger. The drunker they get the more they retreat into those stereotypes, and Mary asks Bigger to sing "Swing low, sweet chariot, Coming fer to carry me home. . . ." Fer, she says. All of it is torture for Bigger, who at the beginning was so impressed with them and so upset that he couldn't stop saying "*yessuh* and *yessum* to white people in one night when he had been saying it all his life long." In the early hours he could not eat with them because under the pressure of their openness he could not chew; it seemed to him "that the very organic functions of his body had altered." As the game goes on he cannot escape the suspicion that they are playing a dreadful game with him, cheating him of the stability, the certainty, that he has learned.

When the Daltons wanted to "give the Negroes a chance," they never reckoned with just how well Bigger would take it. The game that Jan and Mary play throws off his timing. He never wanted to know people like Jan ("He didn't want to meet any Communists. They didn't have any money") and now he has known for too long that whites are not people. "He was sitting between two vast white looming walls." When the walls talk, and ask him, "We seem strange to you, don't we, Bigger?" he replies, "Oh, no'm," and the female wall gets mad. Bigger keeps using the language that's supposed to work, he keeps trying not to be noticed. These whites are cheating; they made up the game and now they're not sticking to the rules. "These people made him feel things he did not want to feel." He has a right to be suspicious; when she gets enough rum, Mary begins to hold him up for amusement. Come, driver, do your tricks.

When he kills, his only way of apprehending that death is: "She was dead: she was white; she was a woman; he had killed her; he was black." It is part of the general stunting of his emotional growth. He later enjoys reports of Japan's war on China and the news that Hitler is "running the Jews to the ground" and Mussolini's troops are slaughtering Spain. There is never any "moral" question for him; aggressions and atrocities are a way of getting out of racial pain. All he wants is some day some black man "who would whip the black people into a tight band and together they would act and end fear and shame." He lives in a world where guilt can only be "a white blur" of blind Mrs. Dalton. (David B. Davis has suggested to me an interesting version, possibly a source, for this central dramatic scene involving Bigger, Mary, and the blind mother. In Thomas Dixon's *The Clansman*, 1905 [on which *The Birth of a Nation*, the first Hollywood spectacular, was based], the insufferable blond virgin, Marion, is raped by the young black man, Gus [the name of Bigger Thomas's best buddy]. The rapist's identity is later discovered by a "scientific" study of his image in the eye of the mother, who watched her daughter's violation.) Guilt is no more than terror; when he sees "the awesome white blur floating toward him" he kills the whiteness.

The murder is an act of creation. It is a way of escaping all the negatives in his life: "The knowledge that he had killed a white girl they loved and regarded as their symbol of beauty made him feel the equal of them, like a man who had been somehow cheated, but had now evened the score." He has had *The Gay Woman*, the pretty white girl who gets drunk. He has taken her out of her high room, brought her down to his own level. He has had her on his bed of coals. Bigger had "committed rape every time he looked into a white face" and now he has done it in a way that the white face would have to cry out in pain. He creates by making whole, by severing the perpetual discontinuity between his two worlds, his aspirations and his abilities to attain their satisfaction; "never had he felt a sense of wholeness" until he introduced Mary Dalton to the furnace.

Murder is a recapitulation of suffering. Bigger hides in empty houses the way Big Boy hid in empty kilns. Bigger wants to know "the right way" to behave when he is captured, "the right way being the way that would enable him to die without shame"—as in *Uncle Tom's Children* Brother Mann and especially Silas in "Long Black Song" and the Negro mother in "Bright and Morning Star" wanted to die. In this sense *Native Son* becomes a way of retrieving the pain of *Uncle Tom's Children*, hurtling that pain into the white community.

But Bigger's act is as futile as was any of the acts in *Uncle Tom's Children* and can bring only the same results. As soon as the newspaper can run the headlines "AUTHORITIES HINT SEX CRIME," Bigger knows it is all over. He has blown the fuse in the white mind. Immediately the police are able to gather three thousand volunteers. "The Negro rapist and murderer" the papers call him before he gets a chance. Massive reprisals come immediately and hundreds of black employees are fired from their jobs, Negro men are beaten on the streets, and all the ghetto hot spots are raided and closed down. The triumph must yet again remain in the mind.

Wright's novel begins to fall slightly out of focus as he tries to show how that triumph registers in his hero's mind. Bigger is smart. The problem Wright did not adequately solve was the nature of Bigger's intelligence. For the most part we see it as a strategic, military mind; he feels power and knows how to use it. But he has no "ideas"—just the vast obsession. He can see the world only as "iron palms" and "fiery furnaces" and a "sea of white faces," blurs of motion and sound and racial horrors. Yet Wright begins to dress up Bigger's "acts of creation" in a prose that rings false. Bigger had "accepted the moral guilt and responsibility for that murder"—but he had not; he could not think in terms of "moral guilt and responsibility," let alone "accept" them. When "a supreme act of will springing from the essence of his being" drove him into crime he "looked wistfully upon the dark face of ancient waters upon which some spirit had breathed and created him." The language is all wrong, and so is Bigger. Preparing for the forensics in the courtroom, Wright begins to lose his grasp on his great character. Able to "look wistfully upon the dark face of ancient waters" Bigger can see a gavel in the courtroom only as a "hammerlike piece of wood."

The problem had been with Wright from the beginning, and all along he had been wrestling with it. In the second section, "Even though Mr. Dalton gave millions of dollars for Negro education, he would rent houses to Negroes only in this prescribed area, the corner of the city tumbling down from rot. In a sullen way Bigger was conscious of this." Wright wants to make his point, then suddenly realizes how important it is that we see it only through Bigger's eyes, and so he leans on "a sullen way" of consciousness. As Bigger climbs in the abandoned house "he remembered that bombs had been thrown by whites into houses like these when Negroes had first moved into the South Side"—yet while Bigger might know that, he does not "remember" it as he climbs inside the old wreck.

The fuzziness in Bigger's characterization is part of a general falling off in the third part as the terms of the book begin to change. Bigger is undergoing a psychic rehabilitation, and too often we see him in his Sunday best: "He lay on the cold floor sobbing; but really he was standing up strongly with contrite heart."

Margaret Butcher has summed up the usual objection voiced against the third part of Wright's novel. "Ideological commitment cheated him of a classic." The Party had interrupted Wright's project and falsified the message of "the bad nigger." Wright himself said in "How 'Bigger' Was Born":

> Two items of my experience combined to make me aware of Bigger as a meaningful and prophetic symbol. First, being free of the daily pressure of the Dixie environment, I was able to come into possession of my own feelings. Second, my contact with the labor movement and its ideology made me see Bigger clearly and feel what he meant. I made the discovery that Bigger Thomas was not black all the time; he was white, too, and there were literally millions of him, everywhere.

Wright seems to want Bigger to stand for any colorless slum kid; his problems are the problems of any impoverished group. Yet in the last section of *Native Son* this idea is only presented briefly and parenthetically in Boris Max's speech. When it makes its second appearance, in the very last scene in the prison cell, Max draws Bigger to the little barred window, shows him the skyscrapers, and says that *that* is what killed you, Bigger, the capitalist economy; the men in those buildings "want to keep what they own, even if it makes others suffer." But Bigger rejects all that. He knows the problems of his life cannot be explained by economics or the class system. Bigger knows, however crudely, what kind of skull he is in.

For the most part, in his lengthy courtroom address, Max takes the terms for granted and speaks solely to the problem of race. What is wrong in the courtroom is not this evasion of the problem by an assertion that "Bigger was not black all the time." Something more generally is wrong with the entire idea of a courtroom confrontation itself. The name "Bigger Thomas" carries us back to the name in that other famous novel which had achieved such immediate and large sales almost a century before. Bigger Thomas is "bigger" than Uncle Tom, but he is part of the family, a son, just as Tom was an uncle. And Wright will use some of Mrs. Stowe's imagery for the Negro in America. The black man is Christ; he is Christ in the complicated way that Buckley, State's Attorney, impulsively feels when he cries, "O suffering Christ, there are no words to tell of a deed so black and awful!" (that is, an inverted Christ). When Bigger is captured, "two men stretched his arms out, as though about to crucify him." The black Christ is nailed by white America. James Baldwin saw

Native Son as "a continuation, a complement of that monstrous legend it was written to destroy," for in Wright's book

> Bigger is Uncle Tom's descendant, flesh of his flesh, so exactly opposite a portrait that, when the books are placed together, it seems that the contemporary Negro novelist and the dead New England woman are locked together in a deadly, timeless battle; the one uttering merciless exhortations, the other shouting curses.

Mrs. Stowe often sacrificed her characters to the moral crusade; the fictional personages became mere pawns in the propagandistic enterprise. The figure of St. Clare is well drawn in the first part of the book, but he tends to disintegrate into merely a mouthpiece for high-sounding morals. That is what begins to happen in Wright's courtroom. Max's speech falls into the category. Mrs. Stowe wrote her book, she said, "to awaken sympathy for the African race as they exist among us," and what else is Boris Max trying to do? Mrs. Stowe showed it by Uncle Tom's gigantic loveliness, concluding we should not do horrid things to people like that. Max shows Bigger's enormous sickness, concluding he is sick because the society is. From exactly opposite directions the two avenues come to the same destination: the crusader tells white America to stop ruining black people.

In the first two parts of the book Wright had been doing something intensely more complicated. We were not seeing Bigger as an object; we were participating with him as a subject. No white man could have written that part of the book, no white man could have stayed so resolutely and utterly in Bigger's brain. But a white man could have written all the courtroom speeches (and it is a white man who gives them). In the last section we are no longer in Bigger's mind. He continues to be the zero he was at the beginning of that third book, a brute in a chair, only listening. Max asks, "Let me, Your Honor, explain further the meaning of Bigger Thomas' life." That is exactly the flaw. I have said the chief virtue of the novel is that it is an exorcism, a calling up of mysterious disasters; the chief error of the third part of the novel is that it is only explanation, no longer a vital artistic effort at a full understanding. What Max is saying is surely true, but it is a truth of a far less demanding kind, the lesser truth that Mrs. Stowe herself achieved.

Your Honor, consider the mere physical aspect of our

civilization. How alluring, how dazzling it is! How it excites the senses! How it seems to dangle within easy reach of everyone the fulfillment of happiness! How constantly and overwhelmingly the advertisements, radios, newspapers and movies play upon us! But in thinking of them remember that to many they are tokens of mockery. These bright colors may fill our hearts with elation, but to many they are daily taunts. Imagine a man walking amid such a scene, a part of it, and yet knowing that it is *not* for him!

All of this is certainly true, not at all an extraneous interpretation of the action. It is a perfectly accurate description of what the action can show us. That is what is wrong. It is an "interpretation." It is part of Wright's flaw of overwriting, a consequence of his fear that we will not see Bigger's meaning, and he must rush in to point it out to us. The third section of the book, all the rhetoric in the courtroom, is the architectural equivalent of the local failures all through the book sentence by sentence, in the unnecessary adverbs and stereotypic figures of speech.

When Bigger is attacked in court, beaten in the head, he is going through a torture that Wright had read about in the Robert Nixon case. On June 8, 1938, Elmer Johnson, the husband of Florence, smashed his fists into Nixon's face at the inquest. Later Nixon rushed Johnson on the stand and tried to strangle him. Thus, at Nixon's trial, and at Bigger's, the courtroom is ringed with uniformed guards to keep the people apart. All of this Wright is able to convey convincingly. But the performance of the lawyer is incredibly stupid—if he is supposed to be a lawyer concerned with getting his man off, and not just a mouthpiece.

> The relationship between the Thomas family and the Dalton family was that of renter to landlord, customer-merchant, employee to employer. The Thomas family got poor and the Dalton family got rich. And Mr. Dalton, a decent man, tried to salve his feelings by giving money. But, my friend, gold was not enough! Corpses cannot be bribed! Say to yourself, Mr. Dalton, "I offered my daughter as a burnt sacrifice and it was not enough to push back into its grave this thing that haunts me."

How Bigger is going to be assisted by this line is utterly unclear.

Those people in the jury box, staring at the father of the lost child, hear her described as a burnt offering; to see Dalton browbeaten will not impel them to leniency. The passage also distracts us and exposes as obtrusive and mechanical the symbols we had lived through with Bigger. It is "poetic justice"—and no other kind—that the Thomas house should be owned by the Daltons. All perfectly true, of course—the philanthropist gouged the rent out of the Negroes and paid them back with ping-pong tables—but we could get that on the pages of the *Daily Worker* and it is an insane tactic in a courtroom. The lawyer turns to the poor blind mother: "And to Mrs. Dalton, I say: 'Your philanthropy was as tragically blind as your sightless eyes!' " Again, the defense attorney is publicly badgering a defenseless *blind* parent weeping for the lost child. The "blindness" of Mrs. Dalton had been a great dramatic touch, for we felt Bigger's fear of it, his sense that she was compensating for it with some supersensory perception that saw into him as other whites could not. Her blindness had been an important key in the plot; she had to be in the room, but unable to see, for the accidental murder to take place. But the critic who praises the book for its symbols ("a constant play on blindness, focused around the figure of Mrs. Dalton but aimed ultimately at the reader") is taking the least demanding of Wright's terms.

When we are pulled up out of the nightmare to this reflection upon it, we begin to ask all the wrong questions. The rum bottle—how does it suddenly appear in court when Jan had left it in the gutter and there was no reason for anyone to start looking for it until several days and several garbage trucks had passed? When the judge calls the lawyers forward and they have a conference at "the railing" for "over an hour" surely in any courtroom the conference would be in the judge's chambers. These are silly little details, hardly worth mention, but they bother us in the third part because we are "shedding daylight" on the problem—we have gone out of Bigger's mind to look back on it—and the book comes to a standstill, where we look at the landscape to see everything out of place. Max is not defending Bigger; Wright is using Max to point Bigger's tragedy out.

Bigger has, as one critic has said, an "incurable neurosis." Or, as Wright himself said, Bigger is "an obscene joke happening." In one sense the courtroom scene is in a line of the finest detective stories and murder mysteries, Wright's attempt to take the step that will lead to greatness. He is trying to expose communal guilt. He is entering on a question of judgment that will judge the whole structure of his work and the moral views we hold of it. We know the community is not going to let Bigger go. Buckley cries, "Your Honor, in the name of Almighty God, I plead with you to be merciful to us!" He is facing an inescapable fact: to say that we may have "made" Bigger what he is, that may be true. But the damage has been done. It has been accumulating and maiming for centuries. But what are the people in that room, facing that Bigger, supposed to do about it? They face a boy who killed twice in twenty-four hours, killed black and white. It becomes a question for the reader. Given the fact that the society into which Bigger would ultimately reenter is not going to be changed, and given the present sad state of psychiatric tools to rehabilitate him wholly, what is to be done? Perhaps the most humane course, though it is a wretched one, is to allow him to live out his life in prison. And this is what Boris Max asks.

But that isn't what *Native Son* is all about. Again the courtroom scene only distracts us from Wright's central vision. Max says, "In a certain sense, every Negro in America's on trial out there today." But that "certain sense" is terribly important, and here in part 3 of his novel Wright has it wrong.

He said in "How 'Bigger' Was Born" that "what Bigger meant had claimed me because I felt with all of my being that he was more important then what any person, white or black, would say or try to make of him, more important than any political analysis designed to explain or deny him, more important even, than my own sense of fear, shame, and diffidence." But "what Bigger meant" had not sufficiently "claimed" him so that he could resist the impulse to "try to make" an explanatory rhetoric that would "deny him." Or, to be fully fair, Bigger had "claimed" Richard Wright in the first two sections of the book to the point of utter possession.

II

In *Black Skin, White Masks,* Frantz Fanon comments briefly on the character of Bigger Thomas. Before the murder of Mary Dalton, Fanon says, "No one knows yet who [Bigger] is, but he knows that fear will fill the world when the world finds out. And when the world knows, the world always expects something of the Negro. He is afraid lest the world know, he is afraid of the fear that the world would feel if the world knew." And so, "Bigger Thomas acts. To put an end to his tension, he acts, he responds to the world's anticipation." And in this sense, killing is not really something Bigger does; it is something he is. An undeniable part of his personality, the act is his mind. All his life he can wait for it to happen to him. Murder is his cultural reality. "He had killed many times before," Wright says, "only on those other times there had been no handy victim of circumstance to make visible or dramatic his will to kill." In such a world, the murder becomes as inescapable as the terms of a logical proposition.

At the beginning of the story Bigger's mother cries out at him, "We wouldn't have to live in this garbage dump if you had any manhood in you." The kitchenette is an assault on his manhood. The squalor is the sign of a submerged manliness, a masculinity so utterly choked off that it wastes away. The slum means every day to his ears and eyes and nose only one thing: White Power. Crazed with black impotence he awakes to find giant rats attacking his women. "He hated his family because he knew that they were suffering and that he was powerless to help them." The utter pity of his dangling the dead rat before the women's eyes is not just that he gets a kick out of scaring them; dangling the rat's body before their eyes he is offering some little proof of his power. See this, I killed it. I am *something* of a man. I can kill.

The scene with the rat establishes in the opening pages the dimensions of the curse and provides for Bigger's murders as a psychic and cultural inevitability. It is not just that the white folks live somewhere on a green hill; when Gus asks Bigger where they live Bigger doubles his fist and strikes his solar plexus: "Right down here in my stomach." To kill the whites is a way, the only way, for Bigger to take "fully upon himself the crime of being black." The two crimes are logical consequences of each other.

Stephen Marcus has written that "one of the principal components in male sexuality is the desire for power, the desire to dominate. In modern society, money is one of the two or three most important instruments of personal power, and the association of sex and money through the medium of power is an inevitable one." It is inevitable for Bigger Thomas: famished in his desire to dominate, frustrated of any means for that domination, his triumph is to "settle at last" the old score through rape and ransom, a violation of the beautiful money-princess in the white castle. That is his only power, bringing the violence home, to invent horror in the horror that invented him. It is his inevitable vocation. Erik Erikson suggests in *Young Man Luther* that "probably the most neglected problem in psychoanalysis is the problem of work. . . . Decades of case histories have omitted the work histories of patients or have treated their occupation as a seemingly irrelevant area of life," and yet "many a delinquency begins by society's denial of the one gift on which a destructive individual's precarious identity depends." Which is exactly the point with Bigger: his power has nowhere to go. The problem is a central one in psychoanalytic study—the way work structures the psyche. For Freud, the individual's relationship to work does not just involve economic security but also the achievement of psychic equilibrium. The question, Who am I? in a capitalistic "democracy" involves and is intimately a part of the question, What do I do? And Bigger cannot *be,* in any constructive way, because the culture in which he lives will not let him *do*—do anything more than stand on street corners. Bigger drifts. He waits. His mind drifts and waits. He moves only in violent fantasies, with nothing other than dreams of destruction to give himself to. Wherever his aggressiveness turns, it is stopped up. His remark on the street corner—"Them white boys sure can fly"—is a literal truth, an axiom; the whites surely can fly and Bigger cannot. He is acknowledging not only their skill but his inability ever to have the chance of attaining it. When Max asks him in the cell what he wanted to be, every desire is one of escape, power, integration of mind and muscle. But it is a Jim Crow army, a navy where blacks wash dishes. Everything in his world equips Bigger to be a soldier of enormous effectiveness. In that sense he is a most useful commodity for the society. He can do its killing. But the culture denies him that "pleasure."

The continuing image of his dilemma is in a sensation of impotence, of falling. Gus says with "uneasy eagerness" to Bigger's premonition that "something going to happen to me . . . something I can't help" that "It's like you going to fall." What Bigger and Gus speak on the street corner comes true in the Dalton bedroom, where the something Bigger can't help is thrust upon him and he feels "as though he were falling from a great height in a dream." It is a dream that tortures him in his last time with Bessie when, as he enters her, "the wind became so strong that it lifted him high into the dark air, turning him, twisting him, hurling him . . . at a moment he could not remember, he had fallen." And when he plays black soldier on the street he cries not just for destruction of the whites but a special destruction—"Look ut the white folks *fall*" (emphasis mine). When he escapes from the Dalton house he hurtles through the window and falls, urinating, in the snow. And when white society captures him on the rooftops, "his body teetered on the edge . . . then he was falling." The white world's phallic power ruins and rips his out; he is finally captured when he is thrown into the air by a burst from the white "hose" that ejects him from his frozen bed.

Bigger is a Native Son. Jean-Paul Sartre has written that racist oppression produces "neither man nor animal" but "the native." Wright's title means more than that he is just American; it means more carefully than that, and means America's possession of him is a special one. For Bigger Thomas to come fully into his title, he must be truly "native" to the land that tells him he must kill. Fanon says in *The Wretched of the Earth* that "the native is an oppressed person whose permanent dream is to become the persecutor" and "the native who decides to put the programme into practice, and to become its moving force, is ready for violence at all times. From birth it is clear to him that this narrow world, strewn with prohibitions, can only be called in question by absolute violence."

It is that perception which redeems the final pages of *Native Son*, where Wright makes a partial recovery from the disasters of the courtroom. Bigger, as a national child, has gone out in the course of the story to seek his manhood. We are the most violent of nations, the country that has found the way to destroy the best. Our heroes traditionally are men of great violence, our Jesse Jameses, and John Dillingers, and Al Capones. Someone once said that our western heroes had to ride white horses because if they didn't, we could not tell them from the bad guys. Native Son is America's child by entering into her murders. If murder is freedom, it is because Bigger is entering into the cliché and living most fully exactly that role white society places upon the Negro. He is the black man's Horatio Alger, the good little bad boy who has a dream and works it out. He is our black Poor Richard, our black Gatsby, and his life is a success story. His greatest success must be a great horror for he finally comes to embody all the junk of the nightmare. It is not a contradiction to call him a "beast of the skull" (a phantom) and to call him also a boy on the ghetto streets, for he is a walking, breathing nightmare, the social fact in its purest form. If a culture works hard enough on the assumption that the black man is a dirty nigger, it is inevitable that a culture of such enormous power will turn some black men into dirty niggers. The final success is to make the myth prowl the streets.

Bigger has heard what the white world will do with him. He has heard Buckley in the courtroom. Fanon has pointed out that the master, the racist colonizer, always refers to his subject in zoological terms. Buckley's courtroom speech is a protracted bestiary, jerking in sadism:

> Every decent white man in America ought to swoon with joy for the opportunity to crush with his heel the woolly black head of this black lizard, to keep him from scuttling on his belly farther over the earth and spitting forth his venom of death!

And Bigger, too, "swoons with joy" when he is able to mutilate the white head. At the very end of the book Bigger shouts that he didn't want to kill. "But what I killed for, I *am!* It must've been pretty deep in me to make me kill!" The ideological spokesman retreats, pleading "desperately," and his eyes are "full of terror." Only young Jan Erlone had been able to convince Bigger of real understanding. (And Jan Erlone is modeled on Wright's real-life friend, Jan Wittenber. "Erlone" is Wright's dialect tribute that, as he said, Jan *alone* among the white comrades was capable of real sympathy.) But at the end of the novel Boris Max can only filter Bigger through the Party's vision. Max can explain Bigger to the white courtroom; alone with Bigger, Max is lost. He murmurs, "no; no; no . . . Bigger, not that. . . ." Bigger, finally, is black all the time.

The agony for Wright at the end of the book is the terror of his terms. The black boy ends up as he began, caged. Wright had opened the door in the forensics of the courtroom, but even that could not pull the beast out. At the end Bigger is simply there—like *The Hairy Ape* in the last scene of O'Neill's play—and in spite of all the ideas Wright has brought forward to retrieve him, Bigger "smiled a faint, wry, bitter smile." Whenever he had thought of murder he "smiled"; after he murdered he "smiled"; and now that smile is all of it, the final excruciating expression of his life.

The achievement of the novel is an understanding of this hate, not an exaltation of it. What is meant by saying that if one lives too long with the beast one can love it is that the mark of one's authenticity becomes the virulence of one's rage. The only "real" Negro is "black crazy." Throughout the novel we are in there with Bigger, feeling in unbearable physical terms the massiveness of his hate. Facing the private detective, Bigger "hated Britten so hard and hot, while standing there with sleepy eyes and parted lips . . . for a split second a roaring noise in his ears blotted out sound." The physical terms are unbearable: he is deafened by his hate and yet he must stand as a colored boy "with sleepy eyes and parted lips"—a hate that cannot be let out in a striking lash, a hate that grows even more unbearable by the absolute necessity of being what the white man expects. Throughout the novel we are continually facing such moments with Bigger, participating with him as he endures them. But we should be rather more accurate than several critics have been in defining our relationship to that feeling. We do not "sympathize" with Bigger. We *feel with* him, perhaps, but we do it in a special way. When Fanon speaks of violence, and the necessity for it, he addresses himself to a revolutionary social situation. "Violence" is impelled by consciousness. The hatred of "the native" is at the service of an idea and his destruction is a necessary prelude to a social creation. Violence is not a helpless reflex, a gross futility, an insane outburst. It is part of the large, communal act: repossession of the African home. But the violent blood baths of Bigger Thomas are at the mercy of the system which engendered them. He hacks his way to a dead end.

Bigger had nothing other than his hate, nowhere to go with it. And America electrocutes her native son when he claims his birthright in the fullness of paralyzing rage.

Bigger's Infernal Assumption

Roger Rosenblatt

The novel which illustrates the cyclical quality of black fiction most dramatically is *Native Son*. The novel is treacherous because it is readily understandable, yet the fact that it is readily understandable, that all its meanings are on the surface, enlarges its power to terrify. The story seems to explain itself as a social document: Bigger Thomas, nineteen or twenty, black, full of unarticulated hate, is hired as a chauffeur by the rich, white Daltons. The Daltons' daughter, Mary, asks Bigger to drive her to a rendezvous with her forbidden boyfriend, a young Communist named Jan Erlone. During the course of the evening, Jan and Mary proceed to overwhelm and confuse Bigger with self-congratulatory gestures which proclaim Bigger's racial equality. When the party breaks up, Mary is drunk, and Bigger must carry her to her room. The blind Mrs. Dalton enters to see if Mary has returned. Bigger, terrified that he will be discovered and falsely accused, pushes a pillow down over the girl's face in order to keep her quiet. Doing so, he smothers her, panics, and in desperation to hide the crime, shoves Mary's body, beheaded, into the furnace. Trying to protect himself, he makes a blundering attempt to cast suspicion on Jan by suggesting that the Communists have kidnapped Mary. He enlists the help of his girl, Bessie, but afraid that she will give him away, he murders her. Bigger is hunted, captured, tried, defended on social grounds, and left to await execution.

From *Black Fiction*. © 1974 by the President and Fellows of Harvard College. Harvard University Press, 1974.

The plot of the novel may be horrifying, but its horror is easily dissipated. Once the sociological explanations of Bigger's behavior have been made, neatly and at length, as they are by his lawyer, Max, that particular level of nightmare, which is the level of action, disappears because the reader feels free of the book's external events as soon as those events have been cleared up by science. When *Native Son* first appeared, its critical acclaim was based on the discovery of its social abstractions. It was considered to be a great and powerful book because it dramatically exposed a series of great and powerful injustices. Only Baldwin differed from most of the critics when he said that *Native Son* was not about injustice, but about the human heart, thereby substituting one abstraction for another.

Native Son is neither about injustice nor the human heart, but about the individual, Bigger Thomas. The novel pivots on a simple exclamation repeated on two occasions by Bigger's mother: "Boy, sometimes I wonder what makes you act like you do." No one in the book gets at the answer to that problem because Bigger lives apart from other people. The outer world, as his author puts it, is "not his world." Bigger's world consists of images, surrealistic distortions of ideas and feelings which grow out of a mind attuned solely to sensations. He is distortion himself: an upside down man who, when he tries to stand right side up, turns inside out.

His life began backward with a geographical inversion. His family traveled north in the "great migration" expecting to realize emancipation, and received instead a different form of enclosure. They escaped out of one house of bondage into a smaller and more cramped house where the story begins. The Thomases moved north to be able to earn a living and began a slow death of mind and body. They moved up to go down. They emigrated to a colder climate where the heat was stifling. Specifically, they undertook a pilgrimage to the promised land of Chicago which turned out to be hell, despite its Loop, its fake ring of paradise. The city was a butcher of hogs, and was known for its fire.

Hell, then, is where *Native Son* is located. The shame which its characters experience is the shame of the damned. Bigger is told to turn to the wall while his sister dresses and undresses because Vera wants to hide her nakedness from him. Bigger does not like people staring at him either, fearing exposure of secret and nameless sins. His home is the hell of *No Exit*:

He looked round the room, seeing it for the first time. There was no rug on the floor and the plastering on the walls and ceiling hung loose in many places. There were two worn iron beds, four chairs, an old dresser, and a drop-leaf table on which they ate. This was much different from Dalton's home. Here all slept in one room; there he would have a room for himself alone. He smelt food cooking and remembered that one could not smell food cooking in Dalton's home; pots could not be heard rattling all over the house. Each person lived in one room and had a little world of his own. He hated this room and all the people in it, including himself.

Bigger wants to become an aviator and join the air force, but he cannot fly. He exclaims, "What in hell can a man do?" meaning what can a man do in hell. His friend Gus says, "God'll let you fly when he gives you your wings up in heaven," but Bigger is not going to get to heaven. He has his "flight" (the title of the second section of the novel), but it only goes from one zone of hell to another. He uses the word "hell" continuously, especially in the presence of Bessie, who shares his hell and has a quieter one all to herself. Mary makes him conscious of his blackness; he thinks, "Goddam her soul to hell," which, in a way, he does by placing her body in flames, but he also suffers hell on her account:

> Why was Mary standing there so eagerly, with shining eyes? What could they get out of this? Maybe they did not despise him? But they made him feel his black skin by just standing there looking at him, one holding his hand and the other smiling. He felt he had no physical existence at all right then; he was something he hated, the badge of shame which he knew was attached to a black skin. It was a shadowy region, a No Man's Land.

And there is Chicago all around, the wider hell from which, like his home, there is no exit: "he could not leave Chicago; all roads were blocked."

As a boarder in hell, Bigger is always close to fire and incendiary material. He is condemned by the State as an "infernal monster." The message he reads from the skywriting plane is "Use Speed Gasoline," potentially useful advice for his burning of Mary. There is a variety of fires inside him: "Bigger laughed, softly at first, then harder, louder, hysterically; feeling something like hot water bubbling inside of him and trying to come out." Whenever he thinks of white folks, "It's like fire," or "Like somebody's poking a red hot iron down my throat." One of his duties in the Dalton home is to tend the furnace and keep the coals glowing. As long as the fire rages Bigger is safe. When the flames die down, Mary's bones and his crime are discovered. At one point Mary says to him, "Got a match? Strike it." During his capture Bigger is shot with a fire hose. "Many times, when alone after Max had left him, he wondered wistfully if there was not a set of words which he had in common with others, words which would evoke in others a sense of the same fire that smouldered in him." A mob burns a cross for Bigger. Bigger is sentenced to "burn" in the electric chair.

In the context of hell, furnaces become the centers of activity. There is the actual furnace that holds Mary's body, and there are the figurative furnaces of Bigger's rage and of the home in which he is forced to live. In order to fit Mary in the furnace Bigger must cut off her head. In order for Bigger, his family and friends, to fit into the furnaces of their own tenements, their heads also had to roll. Mary's decapitation is only the physical counterpart of a neater, more sophisticated and bloodless execution: the action by which a man's head (his intelligence, his source of feeling, aspiration, achievement) is removed so that he may more easily be closeted, categorized, buried, or cremated. Dan McCall (*The Example of Richard Wright*) points out that as an act of symbolic revenge it is only natural that Bigger must always go for the head—for the rat's head at the outset of the novel; for Mary's head; for Bessie's head; for the head of the vigilante hunting him on the roof; even metaphorically for the head of his mother: "Well, don't bite her head off, Vera said." The images of his spiritual decapitation and Mary's real one fuse in a dream:

> Out of the surrounding silence and darkness came the quiet ringing of a distant church bell, thin, faint, but clear. It tolled, soft, then loud, then still louder, so loud that he wondered where it was. It sounded suddenly directly above his head and when he looked it was not there but went on tolling and with each passing moment he felt an urgent need to run and hide as though the bell were sounding a warning and he stood on a street corner in a red glare of

light like that which came from the furnace and he had a big package in his arms so wet and slippery and heavy that he could scarcely hold onto it and he wanted to know what was in the package and he stopped near an alley corner and unwrapped it and the paper fell away and he saw—it was his own head.

The substitution of his head for Mary's is made not only because Bigger had had his "head" removed long before he had actually decapitated Mary, but because by tormenting Bigger with futile and anachronistic gestures of good will, Mary only served to remind Bigger that he had no head with which to receive or apprehend her gestures. To Bigger all such gestures were but dimly perceivable; therefore, his responses to them were mumbles. After centuries of historical decapitation, Mary was saying "think and feel" to a man who had lost his ability to do so.

What does it mean to lose one's head? We are traveling through a hell called heaven, through a labyrinthine kind of madhouse where, in one way or another, everyone has lost his head. There is a great deal of hysteria in the novel: hysteria in a poolroom brawl where Bigger, afraid to go ahead with a robbery of his own design, transfers his fears to his friend Gus and starts a fracas in order to abort the plot; hysteria in Bigger's cell; in the outcries of Bessie and his mother. It is also a feature of this madhouse that everybody in it accuses everybody else of being crazy. Mary's mouthings sound "crazy" to Bigger. Gus, G.H., and Vera all call Bigger crazy. Yet the State's prosecutor, Buckley, will not accept an insanity plea on Bigger's behalf. According to Buckley's definition of justice, and sanity, only a sane and rational man could have committed Bigger's crimes. While depicting the crimes as animalistic and "monstrous," Buckley nevertheless insists upon Bigger's sanity, because if Bigger had been judged insane, his punishment would not have been sufficient. Much of Buckley's effort, therefore, goes into proving the sanity of Bigger's insane crimes, which effort is a form of madness in itself. The only bona fide madman in the novel, one who is officially recognized and certified as a lunatic, is the black intellectual who is thrown into Bigger's cell, who demands his "papers." The irony of his brief appearance is that although he raves and grips the bars of the cell and frightens Bigger and the other prisoners with the outer trappings of lunacy, what he says about having been robbed of life is, in fact, quite reasonable. His madness is identified not by crazy ideas voiced in a sane context, but by the reverse.

In the madhouse people also wear masks. In jail Bigger begins to see Jan "as though someone had performed an operation upon his eyes, or as though someone had snatched a deforming mask from Jan's face." When Bigger has his interview with the Daltons, he sits squirming in the living room, hat in hand, feet shuffling, repeating "sir" and "ma'am." Earlier that afternoon he had torn around the pool room like a lion, but here in the elegant white home, a Wonderland to him, even his huge size, like Alice's, diminishes, and he assumes the face and features of the "house nigger." He wears the mask, in the sense of Dunbar's poem, as a dual means of self-concealment and self-protection.

According to Henri Bergson's theory of laughter, the mask is a comic instrument, a mechanical object imposed on the suppleness and flexibility of the human face. The force of such impositions is the interruption of human momentum or the human form; thus animals are also funny insofar as their movements and behavior are associated with human beings. But in *Native Son*, despite the fact that characters both wear masks and are identified as animals (Bigger variously as an ape, dog, and gorilla; Vera and Bessie as dogs), no humor is produced. Human momentum is broken all the time in *Native Son* (in a wider sense, the entire story is about the breaking of one man's momentum), yet no comedy occurs because we are merely shown the causal conditions of laughter. Between the perception of the comic situation and the comedy itself lies the context which cuts the laughter off. "It's funny how the white folks treat us, ain't it?" says Bigger. "It better be funny," Gus said.

There is no laughter in the madhouse, but there are games. Bigger and Gus play make-believe, one acting out the part of an army general, the other of J. P. Morgan. They simulate a military-industrial complex, and play roles of enormous prestige and power. Yet the joy in their game is also its pathos. Like participants in a minstrel show, they derive their fun from taking on parts which they, as actors and audience both, know can never be realized. Their language can be exaggerated, they can play their parts to the hilt, and they can engage in satire and fantasy simultaneously, because the very freedom of their game is created and encouraged by an external constriction, the fact that their real aspirations will always be relegated to the world of game-playing. Gus will take orders from Bigger in the charade, but not when it comes to robbing Blum's store, not in real life. In real life Bigger is not to be trusted.

The question is, where is Bigger's real life, and how is it to be distinguished from the varieties of unreality in which he lives? Bigger enjoys the world of the movies, not only the movies themselves, but the movie houses as well, which provide the atmosphere of kings in royal boxes (the theater he goes to is called The Regal) and the darkness that makes Bigger inconspicuous. Yet even the movie (dream) house is not safe from Buckley. At the trial Buckley reveals not only that Bigger went to the movies on the day of the murder, but that he sneaked in without paying. Nor is it only Buckley who invades the movie world, but reality as well. One of the films Bigger watches is about Communists and millionaires. The second is *Trader Horn*, about Africa, but Bigger only wants to think about the story about the "smart people," *The Gay Woman*. Gus tells him that "rich, white women'll go to bed with anybody from a poodle on up. Shucks, they even have their chauffeurs." Bigger daydreams:

> Yes, his going to work for the Daltons was something big. Maybe Mr. Dalton was a millionaire. Maybe he had a daughter who was a hot kind of girl; maybe she spent lots of money; maybe she'd like to come to the south side and see the sights sometimes. Or maybe she had a secret sweetheart and only he would know about it because he would have to drive her around; maybe she would give him money not to tell.

The terrible aspect of this conjecture, of course, is that it all, or most of it, comes true. The satisfaction of the daydream perverts the dream into a nightmare. When the movies are over, Gus remarks, "Swell, wasn't it?" Bigger answers, "Yeah. It was a killer."

In the madhouse people do not wish to be looked at, and yet in one way or another everyone is blind, so the fear of exposure is groundless. In all cases but Mrs. Dalton's, blindness is psychosomatic, but like the others, Mrs. Dalton has a spiritual handicap as well as a physical one. A latter day Grandissime, she and her husband, as Max points out, cannot see the malevolent condition which they serve and perpetuate. Similarly, Mary and Jan cannot see the emptiness of their charity. Bessie is blinded by tears and fright. At different times Bigger is blinded by snow, light and rage. In the presence of Jan and Max he feels "transparent," invisible. At the end of the novel Max "groped for his hat like a blind man." The two abstract conceptions which inform *Native Son*, love and justice, are also traditionally blind.

Only one person, Bigger, gains a kind of sight in the novel, but the vision which Bigger gains is also distorted. It is made up of the images that appear when one holds a magnifying glass close to the face, and then moves it further and further away from one's eyes until the picture reflected in the glass comes in at once clearly and upside down. Bigger begins the story seeing everything in a haze. The sight which he eventually achieves is in sharp focus, but out of whack:

> He felt in the quiet presence of his brother, mother, and sister a force, inarticulate and unconscious, making for living without thinking, making for peace and habit, making for a hope that blinded. He felt that they wanted and yearned to see life in a certain way; they needed a certain picture of the world; there was one way of living they preferred above all others; and they were blind to what did not fit. They did not want to see what others were doing if that doing did not feed their own desires. All one had to do was be bold, do something nobody thought of. The whole thing came to him in the form of a powerful and simple feeling; there was in everyone a great hunger to believe that made him blind, and if he could see while others were blind, then he could get what he wanted and never be caught at it. Now, who on earth would think that he, a black timid Negro boy, would murder and burn a rich white girl and would sit and wait for his breakfast like this? Elation filled him.

It is perfectly apt for Bigger to watch Jan and Mary, as he does, through a rearview mirror, because the final understanding which he reaches of Jan and of Mary, of the Daltons, Max, of the entire white world and his relation to it, is completely turned around: "What I killed for must've been good."

Everything is turned around in this way in *Native Son*, even the idea of color. Here darkness, customarily connected with evil, dishonor, or ignorance, offers safety, whereas whiteness is a source of terror. In black fiction generally, white is the color of suffocation, disorientation, deafness, blindness, of threat, of being cornered. It is also the noncolor by which all others, including black, may be swallowed up. In *Beetlecreek*, William Demby cites "the shriveled paleness" of Trapp's soul. In *dem*, William Kelley's Harlem girls chant about a polar bear coming to enslave them. The domineering chef in Claude McKay's *Home to Harlem* prizes the whiteness of his uniform, as does Mr. Watford, the man without feeling, in Paule Marshall's "Barbados" (*Soul Clap Hands and Sing*). Glory, the shrew of Ann Petry's *Country Place*, is described solely by the blondness of her hair. John Grimes (*Go Tell It on the Mountain*) "knew that time was indifferent, like snow and ice." In Wright, white signifies nothingness: "to Bigger and his kind white people were not really people; they were a sort of great natural force, like a stormy sky looming overhead."

Whiteness and fear have, of course, been connected before. Melville explored and theorized about the monumental supernaturalism of the albino whale; Coleridge's nightmare Life-in-Death was "white as leprosy"; Death itself rode a pale horse; and nothing in poetry so conveys the awful sense of blankness as Wallace Stevens's "Snow Man." But there is a difference in such perceptions in black and white literature. In the examples above, and more could be cited, whiteness usually is terrifying only when it is attached to objects already terrible in themselves; whereas in black fiction the fearfulness of white is the rule, not the exception, and is wholly independent of customarily frightening objects. The only instances in which the fearful qualities of the color and the object are cooperative are those where the object concerned happens to be a man (or as in Ellison's "Flying Home," a man wearing a sheet). Among white authors one rarely finds a character to be terrifying, as Bigger finds Mr. Dalton, simply because he is white.

Time, too, is out of joint here, as it is in most of black fiction. Characters such as Constance of Countee Cullen's *One Way to Heaven* and Jake of McKay's *Home to Harlem* cling tenaciously to the present not out of simple hedonism, but because the past and future have no meaning for them. Neither does the act of telling time. *If He Hollers Let Him Go* and *Native Son* both begin with the noise of clocks, but the clocks serve only as instruments of alarm. At the conclusion of his story, Ellison's Invisible Man resolves to live underground, observing that "the end was in the beginning." In his introduction to *Black Thunder*, Arna Bontemps declares, "Time is not a river. Time is a pendulum." Toomer says in "Carma" (*Cane*), "Time and space have no meaning in a canefield."

Wright dealt with this question before *Native Son*, in "Long Black Song," of *Uncle Tom's Children*. In that story Sarah's baby is given a clock without hands as a toy. "But why let her tear your clock up?" asks the white drummer who is about to seduce her.

> "It ain no good."
> "You could have it fixed."
> "We ain got no money t be fixin' no clocks."
> "Haven't you got a clock?"
> "Naw."
> "But how do you keep time?"
> "We git erlong widout time."
> "But how do you know when to get up in the morning?"
> "We just git up, thas all."
> "But how do you know what time it is when you get up?"
> "We git up wid the sun."
> "And at night, how do you tell when it's night?"
> "It gits dark when the sun goes down."
> "Haven't you ever had a clock?"
> She laughed and turned her face toward the silent fields.

The point is that time is only useful when one's life is changed during or by it. When no change occurs, it merely becomes a measurement of stasis, as it is for Sarah. To have clocks and watches around is, in fact, worse than not owning such instruments, because they only serve as reminders of a world in which time does have meaning. This comments obliquely on a world in which a linear conception of history has meaning, a world different from the one Wright is depicting.

Time is out of joint in *Native Son* because a madhouse has no need for time, or accurate time. Bigger has a way of continually forgetting the time. As soon as he earns enough money the first thing he plans to buy is a gold watch that will be completely useless to him. Mr. Dalton begins most of his sentences with "Now" when he usually means "Never." Peggy, the Dalton's cook, wants the household to run like a clock, but Bigger's crime upsets her schedules. When the correct time is known, trouble usually follows. The alarm clock that opens the book signals the entrance of a rat. The timing is off for the robbery of Blum's. In Mary's room the clock with the glowing dial serves as a witness to murder. Bigger's alibi depends on a knowledge of time. When Bigger confesses to Buckley it is observed that "he came through like a clock."

The maddest aspect of the madhouse is the particular crime of which Bigger is accused. It is not murder after all, but rape. Murder, in all other situations, would be the most heinous crime imaginable, especially a brutal murder involving the hacking up of a pretty girl; yet initially the coroner's inquest is desperate to prove, and the State chooses to find, Bigger guilty of Mary's rape ("the central crime is rape"), thereby placing rape above murder in an upside down hierarchy. In a mad context, however, that ranking makes sense, because murder only represents the destruction of white by black, a terminal concern, whereas rape metaphorically represents the assertion of Bigger's black manhood in a white world. The State declares that it is this assertion, as an idea, which is intolerable, and must be punished as the capital offense. Moreover, it must be punished by death because death alone can cancel out the sexual phantasmagoria regarding blacks which the white characters have created out of their wretched imaginations. (At one point even the wretched imaginations get out of hand: "Your Honor, must not this infernal monster have burned her body to destroy evidence of offenses worse than rape?") The white guilt here is enormous, and the main objective of the State is to generate enough hate to neutralize that guilt.

Bigger does not rape Mary, but he might have, at least in terms of the spirit. Mary teased Bigger with her body in the car and as he carried her upstairs, but throughout the evening she had also teased him with her mind: "Why was Mary standing there so eagerly, with shining eyes?" She had said to Bigger, look at me, my big house, my free and extravagant life, and you can have everything you want. Bigger was aroused, in sexual terms, to manhood:

> It seemed that her actions had evoked fear and shame in
> him. But when he thought hard about it it seemed impos-
> sible that they could have. He really did not know just
> where that fear and shame had come from; it had just been
> there, that was all. Each time he had come in contact with
> her it had risen hot and hard.

The sexual terms recur when Bigger begins to experience a number of different passions: "He hated Britten [Dalton's detective] so hot and hard, while standing there with sleepy eyes and parted lips, that he would gladly have grabbed the iron shovel from the corner and split his skull in two." Before the murder, Bigger had been tense; afterward "he felt a lessening of tension in his muscles." And Bessie tells him that they will accuse him of rape:

> Had he raped her? Yes, he had raped her. Every time he felt as he had felt that night he raped. But rape was not what one did to women. Rape was what one felt when one's back was against a wall and one had to strike out, whether one wanted to or not, to keep the pack from killing one. He committed rape every time he looked into a white face. He was a long, taut piece of rubber which a thousand white hands had stretched to the snapping point, and when he snapped it was rape. But it was rape when he cried out in hate deep in his heart as he felt the strain of living day by day. That, too, was rape.

Buckley was right about rape all along, not in fact, but in what he guessed and dimly comprehended: that Bigger had indeed been on the verge of rape that night, on the verge of becoming aware that he had human possibilities. If he had been permitted to live after having committed a crime like that, the State's guilt would have been unbearable.

There can be no guilt in the madhouse, nor can there be any love. Bessie is Bigger's girl, but Bigger, as he readily admits to Max, does not love Bessie. He does not love her, first, because she is, according to an inverted criterion, unlovely. The women who are designated as beautiful in the book are Jean Harlow, Ginger Rogers, and Janet Gaynor, the pinups decorating the wall of Bigger's room in the Dalton house, photographs left there by a black man named Green, Bigger's predecessor. Bessie is not called beautiful; she is merely property. We only learn that she has a family name, Mears, after she is dead. She is owned by the people for whom she cleans house, by the booze that sustains and dulls her, and by Bigger ("You got a girl, Bigger?" Mary asked. "I got a girl," he said), who uses her in bed and, like Corley in Joyce's "Two Gallants," for petty theft. Bessie is a usable commodity not only to the end, but afterward. Even in death her body is essential as evidence.

Bigger is accused of having committed "two of the most horrible crimes in the history of American civilization." The representation of American civilization suits the madhouse well. Wright's definition of civilization is like Thurber's: the wolves eat the rabbits in order to civilize them. Here the civilized include Britten, Buckley, the Daltons and the mob; while the uncivilized, the animals, are the Thomases, Gus, G.H., and Bessie who, partly for their own good, must be hidden away or destroyed. Chief among the civilized are Mr. and Mrs. Dalton, who because of their wealth, position, and especially their professional philanthropy, symbolize the height which a democratic civilization can reach. They pose for the news photographers like the couple in Grant Wood's *American Gothic* and are honored for the American dream which they are and have made.

Yet Bigger, too, has forged an American dream and like McTeague, with whom he has much in common, has done so at great pains, and with much self-sacrifice. In his own version of the American way, he has plotted and saved and pulled himself up by his own bootstraps. The facts that his particular American dream had to be realized in his own dark and separate America, that his America is upside down, and that his dream is a recurrent nightmare do not detract from or lessen the truth that by the end of the novel Bigger has indeed created something very big. In a madhouse as on a frontier, all things are possible. Even murder, says Max, can be an act of creation. If that is so, Bigger the murderer becomes the god of creation. He has created not only an American dream, but his own divinity as well.

Of the twelve Apostles the most mysterious was Thomas. He was devoted to Jesus ("let us also go, that we may die with him," John 11:16), but he was a shadowy, despondent man who believed without joy or hope, and tended toward gloom. He also only trusted in what he could see with his own eyes, and was curiously absent at the resurrection (John 21:19–24). Bigger Thomas is also a dark figure who only believes in what he sees. He too develops a great devotion, but not to another man. Bigger becomes an apostle of himself. The only resurrection he would attend would be his own.

As befits a savior, prophecies attend him on all sides. The political poster on the signboard near his home shows Buckley, running for State's Attorney, pointing his finger directly at Bigger: "If You Break The Law, You Can't Win." Near the end Bigger tells Max, "I knew that some time or other they was going to get me for something. I'm black. I don't have to do nothing for 'em to get me. The first white finger they point at me, I'm a goner, see?" Peggy tells Bigger that his most troublesome task in the Dalton household will be taking out the ashes. The device Wright uses (here and in *Uncle Tom's Children* as well) of describing human actions in terms of the motions of disconnected parts of the body foreshadows Mary's burial. "Stop prophesying about me," Bigger warns his mother, but the prophecies persist, nevertheless. What Bigger will do, what will happen to Bigger, and what Bigger will become are questions on which every life in the novel depends.

It is Max who first hits upon the notion that Bigger's killing of Mary was an act of creation, by which he means that Bigger, who was predetermined to do nothing all his life, had found in the act of murder a way to do something. But Bigger creates more than murder when he smothers Mary. Like Joe Christmas of *Light in August*, he creates himself. There was no rape; Bigger was born of an immaculate conception. In an upside-down world murder becomes a sacred ceremony, and even though this particular nativity was attended by no star shining in the East (the sky was full of snow that night), Bigger himself senses the hallowed quality of the scene. Before decapitating Mary, he pauses "in an attitude of prayer," because he senses that by this act he has accomplished a miracle. He becomes the Father who creates the Son in himself.

Here, then, is the native Son who would make the blind (Mrs. Dalton) to see, the lame (Gus) to walk again, who would purify and cleanse the wicked and ignorant (Bessie), and who would lead the little children (Buddy). Yet Mrs. Dalton clings to her blindness, physical and spiritual; Gus is kicked to the floor of the pool room; the cures Bigger brings Bessie are corruption and death; and at one point he even considers murdering Buddy for fear of betrayal. It is all backward, because Bigger as Jesus is backward. He, too, has his last supper, of bread, but he eats alone. He has not one Judas, but many. All of his disciples would readily betray him. They spread the word, but only of his guilt. Shortly after his birth—the murder—instead of receiving gifts from the three wise men, G.H., Gus, and Doc, Bigger brings gifts, stolen gifts, to them. Unlike his forebear, he resists fiercely on the roof, his mount, and though he is not crucified literally, he is held to await a crucifixion more up to date: "Two men stretched his arms out, as though about to crucify him; they placed a foot on each of his wrists, making them sink deep down in the snow. His eyes closed, slowly, and he was swallowed in darkness."

Bigger is the God of the Old Testament as well as the New. Surrounded by false gods such as the white man's Jesus, he rips what is to him a fake ikon, the cross, from his throat and casts it away. Jan and Mary sing "Swing Low, Sweet Chariot," a slavery song of escape, to him, but Bigger knows that that chariot cannot swing so low as to pick him up and carry him home. He is an all-powerful and vengeful god of a special creation. In his cell, the Reverend Mr. Hammond reminds him of the wonder of Genesis, but that story has no meaning for Bigger. Bigger has had his own genesis, no less wonderful to him that the story of the Bible. "And God saw every thing that he had made, and, behold, it was very good" (Gen. 2:31). "What I killed for must've been good," Bigger declares. "It must have been good."

This final observation of Bigger's is the ultimate inversion. It is the proclamation of a man who has discovered the full meaning of the kingdom of hell. "I myself am hell," said Milton's Satan. Bigger, too, is hell, a hell within the maze of hells around him. His birth in murder was not a second coming but merely one in a thousand such comings, and one, Wright suggests, if nothing changes, which may promise thousands more. If, as Buckley declared, the law is holy, then in the same awful sense of that word Bigger is holy, and so is his ghost. The court clerk asks, "Bigger Thomas will you rise?" The question is rhetorical.

" What Had Made Him and What He Meant": The Politics of Wholeness in "How 'Bigger' Was Born"

Joel Roache

Although it was included in some early editions of *Native Son*, Richard Wright's essay on the genesis of his novel was until recently the virtually exclusive property of specialists who hunted it up there or found it in an anthology of Afro-American writing. With the proliferation of such anthologies (and of the courses that use them) came a wider availability for the essay, and now that Harper and Row have printed it as an introduction to the Perennial edition of *Native Son*, its currency may begin to approach that of the novel. Presumably the essay will be used in the classroom, as it has been used in professional publications in the past, as a source of evidence for various theses about the novel, or to put it more charitably, to "illuminate" *Native Son*. This paper is written out of the conviction that "How 'Bigger' Was Born" merits examination as an important biographical and critical statement in its own right, and that such an examination is necessary to its use in understanding both the novel and the development of Wright's career.

The literary impact of the essay results largely from its dramatization of the creative process as an act of total engagement of the whole person with social reality. Wright attempts to grapple with the social and historical roots of Bigger Thomas as a character and simultaneously with those of his own experience as a person and a writer. This biographical focus, along with the primary reference to one character in one novel, has seemed to obscure the significance of

From *Sub-Stance* 15 (1976). © 1976 by the Board of Regents of the University of Wisconsin System.

the essay for literary history and criticism. Critics have consistently assumed that it falls into already existing historical categories. His reference to people as organisms, for instance, and to himself as "a scientist in a laboratory" are only the most obvious examples of qualities that have made Wright's place in the traditions of American realism and naturalism a cliché in critical discussion of his work. But that observation is rarely brought into direct relationship with the crucial impact of Marxism in Wright's life, an impact which is still another cliché.

The critical literature hardly goes beyond that cliché except to apply simplistically the characteristically dogmatic and frequently time-serving formulas of Wright's contemporaries and to attribute his alleged weaknesses to what Dan McCall has called his "cultural victimization" by the Communist Party. A more sophisticated and sympathetic approach to Wright's own account of his experience as a writer should make a beginning toward a more sensitive awareness of the influence of socialism (which is not identical with the latest pamphlet sanctioned by the Communist Party U.S.A.) upon Wright's work, and also toward a definition of Wright's departures from the assumptions and direction of the familiar traditions of naturalism. I shall suggest, furthermore, that those departures are reflected in precisely the intensely personal quality that is central to the aesthetic satisfaction of reading "How 'Bigger' Was Born."

Since Wright is not attempting to formulate an abstract theoretical construct, the application of particular labels (socialism, dialectical materialism, etc.) is especially difficult and dangerous, mainly because he hardly ever uses them himself. His discussion of the impact of "the labor movement and its ideology," for example, is only two paragraphs long, and only one sentence attacks explicitly the capitalist order: "I sensed, too, that the Southern scheme of oppression was but an appendage of a far vaster and in many respects more ruthless and impersonal commodity-profit machine." Although he does not depend upon such unequivocally political language, however, other passages suggest that the significance imbedded in that rhetoric is nevertheless its thoroughly, albeit unself-consciously, materialistic approach to reality, and especially to the sources of identity. A few paragraphs later he writes of his conviction "that the environment provides the instrumentalities through which the organism expresses itself, and if that environment is warped or tranquil, the mode and manner of behavior will be affected toward deadlocking tensions or orderly fulfillment and satisfaction."

There would seem to be little here to divide Wright from the conventions of naturalism, but it becomes clear from the essay as a whole that he works from a special notion of "environment." Later in the essay, he defines these instrumentalities as the institutions characteristic of a given society; thus Bigger's "fear and ecstasy were naked, exposed, unprotected by religion or a framework of government or a scheme of society whose final faiths would gain his love or trust." His focus on the social instrumentalities for the expression of individual identity is reflected also in his analysis of Bigger's typology. The black person who says, "God, I wish I had a flag and a country of my own" is expressing the need to feel himself as playing "a responsible role in the vital processes of a nation's life" and "to feel the clean, deep, organic satisfaction of doing a job in common with others." Implicit in these passages and underlying the structure of the essay is the conviction that identity is experienced socially in the material world, and this conviction generates the definitive qualities of Wright's perspective and therefore of this thematic and formal approach to his work.

Whereas the naturalist tradition characteristically seeks to render a vision of the human condition that is universal in time and place, cutting through history and across social distinctions, Wright announces his intention to focus on Bigger's experience as a function of his caste and class under specific historical circumstances. He makes it clear that the meaning of Bigger's life is rooted in his exclusion from "the vital processes" of social existence. He recognizes the universal reference in Bigger when he writes of "that part of him which is so much a part of *all* Negroes and *all* whites," but he emphasizes that Bigger "was also a Negro nationalist in a vague sense because he was not allowed to live as an American." And it is "his nationalist complex through which I could grasp more of the total meaning of his life than I could in any other way." So Wright locates the sources of Bigger's divided self in his response to the specific material conditions of his life as a black person. Bigger is divided because he is forced into a "deep sense of exclusion" by a white world: "this intolerable sense of feeling and understanding so much, and yet living on a plane of social reality where the look of a world which one did not make or own struck one with a blinding objectivity and tangibility."

Bigger has been divided from his human aspirations by the operation of that combination of psychological prejudice and economic disadvantage that we have come to call institutionalized racism. So "the look of a world that one did not make or own" implies the existence of others that did make it and do own it, who do participate in the "vital processes" and symbols of solidarity. Thus Lenin strikes a responsive chord in Wright when he shows Gorky "*Their* Big Ben" and "*their* Westminster Abbey" and "*their* library." Wright responds, "That's Bigger. That's the Bigger Thomas reaction." For if there is a "they" who "own" the world, the "one" who does not comes to represent all who do not, becomes an "us." There emerges here an awareness that the obstacles to the achievement of wholeness are inherent not in an abstract human condition but in concrete social structures controlled by specific people, who are therefore responsible. Thus the key terms in the familiar opposition between the world and the self are radically transformed into the oppression of those who do not own the world by those who do.

Each of Wright's descriptions of Bigger's prototypes at the beginning of the essay is informed by this political awareness, expressed in a sensitivity to the uses of power and of the form and symbol of power: wealth. The basic pattern is set by Bigger 1, who uses violence to get control of toys, and then uses the toys to extract humility, a reassurance of his own superiority. It becomes clear later that this superiority is for Wright a substitute for a "scheme of society" to protect him from his "primal fear." The political content of the pattern becomes explicit in Bigger 2; whereas the symbol for the children was toys, for the adult Bigger it is money. Bigger 2 refuses to pay rent or his debts; he does not initiate violence but simply refuses to acquiesce to the reality "that the white folks had everything and he had nothing." It is this identification of a collective enemy that makes his refusal political, and it is predictable that he ends up in prison, a political prisoner in the sense that is fashionable on the contemporary left.

Bigger 3 also refuses to pay, but is a little more aggressive, forcing his way into the movies, and it is appropriate that he escapes prison only by being killed by the protector of white authority, "a white cop." Bigger 4 also rejects the legitimacy of the cash nexus in a situation where others have all the cash when he refuses to dig "ditches for fifty cents a day." But he goes even further and violates "all the taboos," and makes fun of "the antics of white folks" in the bargain. Like the black doctor in *Invisible Man,* he seems not merely bad but absolutely senseless to white society, and he is thus sent "to the asylum for the insane." But just as Bigger 2 is aware of the economic power of the white world, Bigger 4 is conscious of his behavior as a response to the political fact that "The white folks won't let us do nothing." Bigger 5, finally, symbolically sums up the whole pattern when he rides "the Jim Crow streetcars without paying and sat wherever he pleased," rejecting both the power of money and the powers of custom and law, and making it entirely clear that he is prepared for violence in order to continue in this way. Wright is vague about his fate, but if the others are imprisoned, committed or shot, then from what we know (e.g., from *Black Boy* and *Uncle Tom's Children*) about the South of Wright's childhood and youth, lynching is a good guess for Bigger 5.

Each of these prototypes, then, is characterized by the use of violence and money in a conscious pattern of individual resistance to a collective enemy, "white folks," and pays a predictably high price for that resistance and for the sense of identity that it confers. In this regard, however, Bigger is not presented as typical in the usual sense. "I lived the first seventeen years of my life in the South," Wright tells us, "without so much as hearing of or seeing one act of rebellion from *any* Negro, save the Bigger Thomases." But Wright's sense of him as a general type is nevertheless clear in a wide spectrum of behavior which he sees as "variations in the Bigger Thomas pattern." They include the retreat into religion and alcohol and music, a "thousand ruses and stratagems of struggle to win their rights," the pursuit of education and the enjoyment of "the fruits of it in the style of their bourgeois oppressors," right on up to leadership in the community. Hardly anyone is excluded from Bigger's constituency; he is the representative man.

Wright gives other examples to show that his rebelliousness is simply an exceptional expression of a shared impulse. First there is the black person who has moments of intense desire not "to live this way," but unlike Bigger's his anger passes and he "goes back to his job." Then there is the wish for a "flag and a country of my own," but that mood also "would soon vanish." For these people Bigger's anger gets submerged "in the tense grind of struggling for bread," but while they may not share his need for overt rebellion, they certainly share the political awareness out of which it arises. There is expressed here and in those who "praise what Japan is doing in China" and even "say that maybe Hitler and Mussolini are all right; that maybe Stalin is all right" a conscious rejection of what Marcuse has called a one-dimensional world, a world where the conditions of the status quo are taken as given and inevitable. These typical Negroes live with a perpetual awareness of the potentiality in themselves of different conditions, a second dimension where they cease to experience the duality implicit in their exclusion from the dominant culture and live as whole persons. But this potentiality remains abstract, a subjective fantasy overwhelmed by the "blinding objectivity and tangibility" of the world that oppresses them. The importance of the drama of fascism and Stalinism is that it seems to embody a concrete realization of that other dimension.

Similarly, Bigger himself is recognized by his own people as an expression of their desire for wholeness. "We longed to believe and act as he did," Wright tells us; and when Bigger defies the white man, the other "Negroes experienced an intense flash of pride." If Bigger were simply a freak, however admirable for anyone who shared his frustration, he would scarcely provide any occasion for optimism; he would have no prophetic value. So Wright is at pains to show us that besides the typical desire for wholeness that he shares with all the oppressed, his exceptional qualities are not random aberrations, but a "socially conditioned distortion," to use Lukács's phrase, of the norm. He becomes a rebel because he is "estranged from the religion and folk culture of his race," and because he is "trying to react to and answer the call of the dominant civilization." Far from being accidental, "his emergence as a distinct type was inevitable." And only the prediction of the spread of the conditions that produced Bigger is necessary to see in him "the outline of action and feeling which we would encounter on a vast scale in the days to come."

Wright attributes to black people, then, a psychological and intellectual equivalent to class consciousness. His materialism, the awareness of identity as experienced through material conditions and social structures, and his awareness of collective experience, the conviction that the oppressed struggle consciously for identity against the conditions and structures that divide them, converge in a sense of history and society that does not merely explain Bigger, but legitimizes him as a potentially progressive historical force. "The conditions of life under which Negroes are forced to live in America" are "what had made him" and the degree to which he represents "the embryonic prefigurations of how a large part of the body politic would react under stress" is "what he meant," making him a "prophetic symbol."

The biographical importance of the essay begins to merge with its significance for literary history and criticism in this sense of history, which finds value in Bigger's life and therefore in Wright's own. The identification between the author and his character is apparent in more than the logical construct that they share the same background, that if Bigger is typical of black people then he must represent forces at work in Wright's life. "The extension of my sense of the personality of Bigger," he writes, "was the pivot of my life." And the same ideology that helped him to see Bigger clearly also revealed "a struggle in which I was involved." Bigger also becomes central in his developing artistic vision and method. Listening to white writers, he would "translate what they said *in terms of Bigger's life*" (emphasis mine) until their techniques "become *my* ways of apprehending" the life of black people. Listening to Bigger's adulation of Garvey's symbols of nationalist solidarity, "I knew the truth of those simple words from the facts of my own life." His understanding of Bigger helped him get in touch with his own alienation and formulate his response to it: "made me feel more than ever resolved toward the task of creating with words a scheme of images and symbols whose direction could enlist the sympathies, loyalties, and yearnings of the millions of Bigger Thomases in every land and race." And although he hopes to approach Bigger "like a scientist in a laboratory," he must first accomplish "this much knowledge of myself and the world" in order to render "his way of life and mine."

The most important expression of Wright's identification with Bigger is in his response to the anticipated reactions of readers. "I'd be reacting as Bigger himself reacted," he tells us: "I'd be acting out of *fear* if I let what whites would say constrict and paralyze me." And in the following sentence he shows that the writing of the novel functioned for him much as violence serves Bigger: "As I contemplated Bigger and what he meant, I said to myself: 'I must write this novel, not only for others to read, but to free *myself* of this sense of shame and fear. . . .' The writing of it turned into a way of living for me." And he restates the same theme later in connection with the actual work of constructing the novel: "That is writing as I feel it, a kind of significant living."

The identification is made explicit in the "two events" that "made me sit down and actually start work on the typewriter." His work in the South Side Boys' Club gives him an intense experience of the conflict between his needs and the demands of a hostile world. "I felt

I was doing a kind of dressed-up police work, and I hated it," and he empathizes with the black youths to whose demand for life "the police blotters of Chicago are testimony." In this way he allows himself "vicariously, to feel as Bigger felt—not much just a little, just a *little*—but still, there it was." The language of the often quoted passage which follows on the reception of *Uncle Tom's Children* shows the parallel between Wright's motives and Bigger's. "Go to it boys!" he had said at the Club; "Show that full-blooded life is harder and hotter than they suspect." Now he discovers that *Uncle Tom's Children* was "a book which even banker's daughters could read and weep over and feel good about. I swore to myself that if I ever wrote another book, no one would weep over it; that it would be so hard and deep that they would have to face it without the consolation of tears."

It is evident that Wright experienced the writing of *Native Son*, then, as a mode of self-expression and a demand for social recognition parallel to Bigger's violence, a breaking out of his isolation and an attempt to force recognition of his own existence. Indeed, a similar motive is apparent for "How 'Bigger' Was Born" itself when Wright tells us "that his dignity as a living being is challenged by something within him that is not understood." In this need for confirmation of his identity in a world that denies it, Wright reveals his writing as his own "variation in the Bigger Thomas pattern." But at another level, the variation comes still closer to identify with Bigger, because both are engaged in an attack on things as they are. The only difference is that Wright is conscious of his role as an agent of historical change. But the self-actualizing meaning of Bigger's life is the same for Wright as its meaning for Bigger. The only difference is that Wright can articulate that meaning because he connects it with collective experience within the framework of an understanding of history as a dynamic process. The intense personal excitement that informs the essay is a function of this identification with Bigger as black, as oppressed, and as rebel.

That identification is also the source and symbol of the identity between his role as artist and his needs as a social person. The classic writers of realism and naturalism could not achieve such identity because they saw specific interactions between characters and their social environment as metaphors for archetypal conflicts that could be resolved only by flight from social reality or by reference to a moral order transcending that reality. Human aspirations in this literature remain beyond "orderly fulfillment and satisfaction" in the material world. Dreiser, for example, detaches himself from both Hurstwood and Carrie and sees them as simply opposite poles of the same universal, timeless process; similarly, he speaks from outside of Cowperwood's experience and resigns himself to a cosmic equilibrium in social affairs analogous to that which he finds in the biological realm. Other American writers may seem less explicitly detached, but Huckleberry Finn, like Leatherstocking before him, can experience freedom only by lighting out for the territory. And Silas Lapham can achieve a sense of moral worth only by a renunciation of self-realization in the social and material world, a renunciation of the status and wealth that are the only forms of recognition offered by that world. The irony in the title of *The Rise of Silas Lapham* reflects the dichotomy between selfhood and the physical world that goes back in the Western tradition all the way to Zeno at least. Wright makes a departure from that tradition when, by bringing the insights of "the labor movement and its ideology" to bear upon his own life, he sees the possibility of resolving that duality.

Ralph Ellison has held that Wright was the victim of the "much abused idea that novels are weapons and that people with "a commitment to social reality . . . should abandon literature for politics." The importance of "How 'Bigger' Was Born" is that it renders a world of meaning where the concept of the novel as a weapon is not "abused," but used to abolish the fragmentation of consciousness implicit in the separation of art from society, its complexities, contradictions, and development. It is a measure of Wright's integrity as an artist, furthermore, that this world of meaning emerges directly from his structuring of his personal, social, and imaginative experience. In his introductory paragraphs he eschews handy formulas to explain the inexplicable, stating simply and candidly his own need for the recognition and understanding of his experience. Then he gives us the typology underlying his hero's character before mentioning any ideology. This accomplished, he moves into Bigger's historical significance before even beginning to deal with his own particular problems as artist, more than fourteen pages into the essay. The last half then moves forward through the interplay of personal experience, social meaning, and artistic technique, so that that interplay itself renders an artist significance as important as any conclusions that he may draw from it.

The first part of the essay modulates between images of the type and the conditions which produced it. His attempt to "indicate more precisely the nature of the environment that produced these men" quickly goes beyond the "two worlds" of Dixie into history, all the way back to its "imperialistic tug" that dragged black people to this continent. In this way the development of a divided world and a divided consciousness as a function of a specific historic experience is established at the very beginning. A brief catalogue of the categories of personality resulting from that experience then leads up to the first turning point in the essay, his perceptions of the causes of the emergence of Bigger as a special category. These are, first, estrangement from the normal compensations for a one-dimensional reality available to black people, and secondly, a longing for the better life perceived as available to "the dominant civilization." The examples, mentioned above, of this sense of another dimension conclude the first part of the essay.

The pivot upon which we turn into the second section is the point where Wright tells us that he began to focus on Bigger when he came "into possession of my own feelings" and made "contact with the labor movement and its ideology." His new understanding of the conditions which produce Bigger allows him to introduce his broadest statement of the discovery of the forward motion implicit in those conditions, "the possibilities of *alliances* between the American Negro and other people possessing a kindred consciousness." There follows more play with "the concrete picture and the abstract linkages of relationships" which extend finally to white people as well as black. At this point in the essay the direction of the dialectic has been established, and Wright sums it up in three paragraphs of "how I culled information relating to Bigger from my reading." The first example is the conversation between Lenin and Gorky cited above, preceding the paragraph that begins with the "deep sense of exclusion" that they share with Bigger and ends with Wright's sense of "revolutionary impulse." The next example then refers to the forms of expression taken by that impulse on different levels of abstraction. He hears in the rhetoric of "We must be ready to make endless sacrifices if we are to be able to over throw the Czar" a collectivization of Bigger's feeling when he tells a white man, "I'll kill you and go to hell and pay for it." Both are the "tragic calculation of how much human life and suffering it would cost a man to live as a man in a world that denied him the right to live with dignity."

These three paragraphs embody artistically the central theme of the first half of "How 'Bigger' Was Born": the roots of *Native Son* in

social history. The structural direction is clear, moving from examples of alienation (Lenin, Bigger) to an abstract definition of that
alienation and a statement of Wright's conviction of the consequent
thrust toward wholeness; then there is a descent down the ladder of
abstraction from a collective to an individual expression of that thrust.
Wright also introduces explicitly in the structure of this passage the
essential intellectual strategy that underlies the entire essay. Lukács
observes that "The difference, both in historical content and psychol-
ogy, between close-to-life spontaneity and the capacity of generaliza-
tion . . . runs right through history," and that it is the task of the
novelist (as well as of the political leader) to make the connections
between the two. It is evident that Wright sees himself in such a
connecting role, mediating through his craft between on the one hand
Bigger, whose experience he has shared, and on the other the
understanding of history which he has derived from that experience
through the constructs of Marxist ideology.

The process continues in the next passage where he sees in
accounts of Nazism a working out of the implications of Bigger's
response to leaders such as Marcus Garvey. "But more than
anything," he tells us, "*as a writer* I was fascinated by the similarity of
the emotional tensions of Bigger in America and Bigger in Nazi
Germany and Bigger in old Russia" (emphasis mine). This passage
also makes clear the limits of Wright's socialist faith, his recognition
that the need for dignity, for making the dream of a whole life real in
the material world, could lead to "either Communism or Fascism."
What remains of the lessons of Marxism is the sense of history that
sees in that need and the impulse toward revolt that grows out of it
"the potentialities" that determine history, or in Lukács's phrase,
"the objective course of events." And with that recognition he
concludes the first half of the essay and turns to the specific
experiences and problems of writing the novel.

The second half of the essay can be divided into two main
sections. The first deals with the obstacles Wright experienced to
actually beginning work and the considerations and events that helped
him overcome them. The second section then finally goes into the
specific problems of actually writing the novel. We have already seen
that his conviction of Bigger's (and his own) role as historical agent
gave him the strength to defy the anticipated gloats of white readers,
overcoming his own fear and that of black readers as well. In his
response to his "own white and black comrades in the Communist

party" he demands "the right of a man to think and feel honestly." In "fulfilling what I felt to be the laws of my own growth" Wright demands that the Party fulfill in its means "the collectivist and proletarian ideal" which he shared as its end.

Having dealt with his audience, Wright then returns to his character, recalling and clarifying in a few paragraphs the almost intimidating complexities that derive from the analysis that he made in the first half of "How 'Bigger' Was Born." Then in the passages about the South Side Boys' Club and the response to *Uncle Tom's Children,* he again embodies in concrete personal experience the social sources of his artistic motivation. These anecdotes, in turn, set the scene for the final pivotal statement where he renders the fusion of his social vision and his artistic practice. He both refers back to the central thrust of the first half of its essay and looks forward to the technical concerns of the last half of this sentence: "so, when the time came for writing, *what had made him and what he meant* constituted my plot." The entire essay up to this point prepares us to understand this statement, and the language of the last section reinforces repeatedly his assumption of the social roots of his art.

Artistic terms and terms of social reference are repeatedly used interchangeably. Thus the "test-tube" arranged for Bigger is a "social reality or dramatic situation," because "Life had made the plot over and over again." When he begins to get into that reality "American police methods of handling Negro boys" are described as a "stereo-typed situation." And "a unified sense of background" is composed of "the forces and elements against which Bigger was striving." The assumptions implicit in this use of language throughout this culminating section of the essay reinforce the explicit sense of the artist as intermediary between Bigger and the world, the filament through which the meaning of the life of the oppressed passes and is made available to any audience who decides to listen. His gathering "in facts and facets" and holding them until "a new and thrilling relationship would spring up" parallels his earlier account of the process of connecting various levels of abstraction in the ideological realm. This commitment to "where he came from and what he meant" also takes precedence over mere verisimilitude, and justifies his "stepping in and speaking outright on my own," articulating, out of his capacity to generalize, the meaning of Bigger's spontaneous response to his experience.

From this thematic and structural analysis of "How 'Bigger' Was

Born," then, we can abstract a vision of society, and of the artist's relationship to it, that can be summed up something like this: the consciousness of any individual is the product of the interaction between the essential human need for self-realization and the conditions of one's historical position, conditions determined by one's class and/or caste and by the time in which one lives. The writer's ability to articulate consciousness depends upon his sensitivity to individual experience, including his own, in the material and social world as typical of the collective experience of a historically defined group. Wright refers to this sensitivity in the beginning of his essay as "his emotions as a kind of dark and obscure designer of . . . facts." It is with "his emotions," the sense of life intuited from his total experience, that he knows and feels "so much." The novel is the product of the struggle between that knowledge and "the blinding objectivity and tangibility" of the world, a struggle not to create a higher truth that transcends that world, but to discover and render the truth known and felt to be within it as "embryonic prefiguration" of the future.

The "dispossessed and disinherited" contain that prefiguration because they begin from a common sense of exclusion which bifurcates identity; but they are forced to deal with that exclusion as individuals. Their modes of coping and resisting are Wright's "variations" and "shadings" of the Bigger model. That model is seen by the socialist as a "prophecy of our future" because it contains the determination to resist that, collectivized, can force a change. Thus Bobby Seale begins by trying to organize Bigger, the lumpenproletariat, the "brother on the block," and if as John Reilly has suggested, Wright has transformed rage into art, it remains rage nonetheless. But it can become collective only when there is a shared sense of an alternative social model, alternative "instrumentalities" for the organism to express itself, which can be taken for the common goal. The resistance can then be successful in creating those alternatives when there is the shared sense of strategy and tactics that constitutes that elusive but necessary quality in any political movement, discipline.

Wright sees the "childish ideas" of nationalism as a facile and phony response to these needs. The trappings of flag, office, nationhood, provide the illusion of self-realization without the substance; and the charisma of "the leader" as a substitute for a collectively determined and understood strategy. National Socialism and Hitler are the obvious paradigms, and Fanon has analyzed these fascist temptations in *The Wretched of the Earth*. If Wright was unable to effectively dramatize the collectivist alternative, it was not because an understanding of that alternative is not a viable perspective from which to organize material into fictional form, but because he had never experienced that perspective concretely. He had before him a vast panoramic model of where Bigger came from, and Marxism provided the framework upon which to organize his perceptions and experience of that model. But the seeds of the future were deep within the womb of the present, and what Bigger might mean beyond the rebellion necessary to his dignity as a person, remained relatively abstract and elusive to the imagination of even the most creative realist. The only possible opportunity he might have had for such experience was the Communist Party, and the failure of the Party's undemocratic centralism to realize its collectivist ideals in its own practice, its own style of work, is legendary. In a very real sense, Wright's artistic "failure" (say, as a socialist realist) reflects the political failure of the Party. "Success" would inevitably have meant the revolutionary romanticism that plagued most proletarian fiction in the thirties.

The difference that this understanding of "How 'Bigger' Was Born" makes in our perspective on *Native Son* is very subtle, at first glance even slight, but nevertheless profound. The traditional response to Bigger's acts can be represented by Dan McCall's judgment that his violence is "a helpless reflex, a gross futility, an insane outburst." Bigger's conduct is legitimized only insofar as it is understood as an inevitable consequence of his experience. Such an approach attributes to Wright an identification of cause with value typical of the naturalistic, positivist tradition: an "evil" act ceases to be evil when we understand its causes. We forgive the individual who commits the act and dedicate ourselves (perhaps) to eliminating those causes. The individual himself ceases to be evil and becomes merely pitiable. Clyde Griffiths, in Dreiser's *American Tragedy,* is perhaps the best example.

Bigger is of course somewhat less passive than Clyde, and it has been generally understood that his murders constitute acts of personal creation, making possible the discovery of identity. An attempt has been made, furthermore, to socialize that value by the application of constructs from existentialism, a perspective which Wright himself embraced later in his career. The best known recent example is Edward Margolies's *The Art of Richard Wright,* which argues that Wright's major achievement is the creation of a "metaphysical revolutionary." Camus is quoted to show that "The metaphysical revolutionary challenges the very conditions of being—the needless suffering, the absurd contrast between his inborn sense of justice and the amorality and injustice of the external world." Through his violence Bigger rejects that world and "becomes his own god and creates his own world in order to exist." Such a formulation describes with considerable accuracy Bigger's subjective experience, and Margolies is still more exactly correct when he shows that "In an absurd, hostile world that denies his humanity and dichotomizes his personality, Bigger has made a choice that has integrated his being."

Margolies's fundamental assumptions, however, the basic terms of that integration, are diametrically opposed to those developed in "How 'Bigger' Was Born." We are presented again with the old absolutes of the self and the world, defined once more as an "absurd contrast." And the resolution of the conflict is exiled once again to the realm of the "metaphysical." In this way the caste and class basis of Bigger's experience is obscured and he becomes "so much like us." This approach, despite the accuracy of its results on one level, is in sharp contrast to Wright's own vision of identity as the result of the interaction between the self and the world, and of the world as the product of developments in material conditions and social institutions. In Marxist terms, Wright's vision is not absolute, but dialectical; not metaphysical, but materialist. But it is also a mistake to assume that "Max's Communism is of course what Wright presumes his novel is expressing." Wright is perfectly aware of the "irresolution of philosophical attitudes" which Margolies perceives. "How 'Bigger' Was Born" makes it clear that the Negro nationalism, the communism, and the need for identity which both McCall and Margolies analyze so successfully are all present in the environment which helped condition Bigger and in Bigger himself. That he did not choose one of them for the sake of a consistent political perspective or a consistent aesthetic surface expresses his commitment to a critical realism rather than to proletarian romanticism or existentialist modernism.

The existentialist approach, then, while it seems to extend the value of Bigger's experience, is able to do so only by leaping away into the vast abstraction of "the human condition." The consequence is a failure to recognize Wright's vision of that value in the concrete, social world. The difference between the world of meaning created by "How 'Bigger' Was Born" and that in which Wright's critics have operated is clear from McCall's concluding reference to Fanon's "Concerning Violence," which analyzes the therapeutic value of violence for the oppressed in detail:

> When Fanon speaks of violence, and the necessity for it, he addresses himself to a revolutionary social situation. "Violence" is impelled by consciousness. The hatred of "the native" is at the service of an idea and his destruction is a necessary prelude to a social creation. Violence . . . is part of the large communal act: repossession of the African home. But the violent blood baths of Bigger Thomas are at the mercy of the system which engendered them. He hacks his way to a dead end.
>
> (*The Example of Richard Wright*)

But Fanon makes quite clear that the revolutionary impulse of "the native" exists before it is enlisted in the service of any idea, indeed, that it precedes "consciousness." A major purpose of *The Wretched of the Earth* is to analyze how that impulse *becomes* collective, not to argue that it spontaneously serves a "large communal act." Similarly, the central thrust of "How 'Bigger' Was Born" is precisely that Wright sees America itself as on the brink of a "revolutionary social situation" and that Bigger's individual "dead end" may signal a new, albeit ambiguous, collective beginning.

The strategies adopted for this essay may tend to obscure the very real ambivalence which Wright felt about his material, and to push aside somewhat too roughly his aspirations to the status of artist as universal spokesman which he later claimed in *The Outsider* and other works written after he achieved fame, affluence, and expatriation. They may also seem to turn Wright the imaginative writer into a consciously intellectualizing ideologue. But if the label dialectical materialism seems to be applied a little glibly here, it is as a corrective to a critical tradition that has patronized Bigger, or else turned away from him with a revulsion unwarranted for anyone not threatened by the active resistance of the "dispossessed and disinherited," the wretched of the earth. I have also attempted to make clear the degree to which Wright's experience as an artist at this stage of his career constitutes a departure, however temporary, from the direction of most of the other classics of contemporary Western literature. We see Wright attempting to return art to its place as an expression of real social forces, to end its isolation, detachment, and schizophrenic despair, its wallowing in alienation or attempting to transcend alienation without facing squarely its social roots in oppression and exploitation. For the meaning of Bigger Thomas in Wright's life, as a person and as an artist, is summed up in his own summary of Bigger's birth as a character: "The most that I could say of Bigger was that he felt the *need* for a whole life and *acted* out of that need; that was all."

The Beginnings of Self-Realization

Michael G. Cooke

Richard Wright's *Native Son* evinces a remarkable number of likenesses to *Their Eyes Were Watching God,* including coming to a conclusion with a formal murder trial and a personal scene of human reconciliation that yet leaves the protagonist in a state of solitude. Bigger Thomas, moreover, begins under a threat of self-cancellation and is seduced by materialism and then by images, in the pattern held up before Janie. But where Janie naively begins in a corner of the white world and contracts from there into the black enclave of Eatonville and further into "De Muck," Bigger expands out from the ghetto into the white world and beyond that into the levels where social philosophy and political power are struggled over. The difference in scale is significant, not least because *Native Son* puts the figure of solitude— saved however traumatically from self-cancellation and materialism and its sequel, image-worship—into a public position, whence the kind of representative encounter is possible that the domestic concentration of *Their Eyes Were Watching God* in itself precludes.

Bigger Thomas's experience represents a series of violent swings between self-cancellation and self-assertion, with the urgency of his moods of self-cancellation gradually diminishing while the lucidity and control of his self-assertion correspondingly grows. The opening scene of the novel cryptically blends self-cancellation and self-assertion. The context is oddly Hamletic. The "light tapping in the

From *Afro-American Literature in the Twentieth Century.* © 1984 by Michael G. Cooke. Yale University Press, 1984.

thinly plastered wall," the presence of a creature that is shifting and invisible ("I don't see 'im") and the pervasive sense of dread all suggest the visit of the ghost with the message that something is rotten in the state. At this juncture the rot seems all domestic, symbolized as much by the rat that invades and haunts the Thomas family's one-room life as by the mother's telling her first son she wonders why she had ever "birthed" him. The son, Bigger Thomas, clearly dreads and abominates the rat as much as any of them, but once he kills it his hysterical cursing turns into a mixture of vicious play and macho display—he holds the fearful creature toward his sister, and she faints.

The fear Bigger shows toward the rat is involuntary; his attack on his sister is quite voluntary and represents an effort to recover and reestablish himself. But in actuality he has been the one the family has turned to and depended on for protective action. Far from being hostile, they are implicitly complimentary (his younger brother looks up to him with feelings next to idolatry, and his mother cries him down in proportion to her obvious high hopes for him). Why then is Bigger so hostile and self-assertive? The episode with the rat seems less a symbol than a catalyst for feelings of helplessness and worthlessness that Bigger has carried unexpressed for some time. It is a sort of uprising against such feelings that causes him to disappoint his mother and distress his sister:

> Vera [his sister] went behind the curtain and Bigger heard her trying to comfort his mother. He shut their voices out of his mind. He hated his family because he knew that they were suffering and that he was powerless to help them. He knew that the moment he allowed himself to feel to its fullness how they lived, the shame and misery of their lives, he would be swept out of himself with fear and despair. So he held toward them an attitude of iron reserve. . . . And toward himself he was even more exacting. He knew that the moment he allowed what his life meant to enter fully into his conscious, he would either kill himself or someone else. So he denied himself.

It is striking that Bigger, who here suspends all reactions in order to keep from killing, goes into "a deep physiological resolution not to react to anything" *after he kills and is captured*. The apparent identification of not feeling and not killing does not stand up under scrutiny.

Killing does not release feeling in any basic way, but merely rebounds into not feeling, into not daring to feel. This result has in it less paradox than meets the eye, in that the killings are not undertaken out of an uncontrollable upsurge of feeling, but as a way of stifling feeling. When Bigger identifies himself with the act of killing, then, we need to take close account of two facts: (1) to acknowledge the killing is to go past the mere act and the ensuing "physiological resolution not to react," into a stage of open awareness and responsibility; and (2) to accept this stage is to defeat the numbing depression that kept him from himself, his family, and his society, and thus it entails the beginning of his active humanity. It is his ability to *face* the killing, not merely to *perform* it, that counts most in the end. The performance is in itself a reflex of the self-cancellation that marks Bigger at the outset.

Wright sets forth without mercy the state, and the cause, of self-cancellation. He brings home in a radical philosophical way what may have looked like a physical reflex in Janie, or an animal impulse in the cornered rat, namely, the siamese continuity between self-cancellation and a drive to undo others, or murderousness. "Naw; it ain't like something going to happen to me. It's . . . like I was going to do something I can't help." A passive-aggressive seesaw is manifest even in the approach to the holdup; Bigger feels "like a man about to shoot himself." In relation to the job interview he has with Mr. Dalton, Bigger's sister chides him: "you know how you can forget," but it is his very ability to forget that keeps him at the minimum level of stability he exhibits. "Forgetting" essentially means that he suspends "the way he lived; he passed his days trying to defeat or gratify powerful impulses in a world he feared."

The foundation of such a response in the self-protective realities of the human psyche is easy enough to recognize. We may also note that Wright records identical feelings in his own family, in his own life. The situation, with his mother on her deathbed, is admittedly extreme, by contrast with the "normal" signs of weakness and inadequacy in the Thomas household. But the weight of repetition would seem to aggravate the "normal" into the intensity and finality of dying. Here is the pertinent passage from *Black Boy*:

> Once, in the night, my mother called me to her bed and told me that she could not endure the pain, that she wanted to die. I held her hand and begged her to be quiet. That

night I ceased to react to my mother; *my feelings were frozen.* (emphasis mine)

Clearly Wright in the emotional realm matches his mother's position in the physical: he cannot endure the pain. She dies, according to the dictates of nature. He makes himself as good as dead, according to the demands of his spirit. Seeing the same reaction in Bigger gives us important if paradoxical evidence of his sensitivity and makes plausible his eventual emergence, or rebirth, from the extreme of self-protection that causes him to kill Mary Dalton and Bessie Mears, as he has earlier metaphorically killed himself.

It is clear that Bigger's response to self-cancellation early in the novel portends his homicidal behavior with Mary Dalton and Bessie Mears (we must remember that Bigger dreads Mary from the start— "*Goddamn that woman!* She spoiled everything!"—so that his near-discovery by Mrs. Dalton in Mary's room aggravates an already hostile attitude). But this gives the novel, and Bigger's life, an unduly dark fatalistic cast and favors the view of the attorney Boris Max, which Bigger himself rejects. The novel in fact urges us from the outset to see Bigger as more than a defiant and negative character just spoiling for a chance to do harm. The powerful impulses he wishes to gratify must also be taken into account, for though these do not necessarily exclude killing (himself or others), they go far beyond that.

Bigger's notions of positive gratification are not spontaneous and, as it were, age-old, like the nubile Janie's hankering after sunup and pear-tree blossoms and the kisses of the first youth strolling by. They are in their way sophisticated, secondary notions, stemming from sociocultural observation and from the media ("he tried to decide if he wanted to buy a ten-cent magazine, or go to a movie.") The advertising plane that banners USE SPEED GASOLINE brings out Bigger's response to what he sees in actuality and what the media inspire him to conceive: "[White boys] get a chance to do everything"; "I *could* fly a plane if I had a chance"; "Send your men over the river at dawn and attack the enemy's left flank." It soon becomes clear, in the first encounter with the Daltons, that Bigger is as much governed by *images* as by desire for material comfort; materialism and image-worship, which occur discretely in *Their Eyes Were Watching God,* overlap here, and complicate Bigger's responses. In the Daltons' neighborhood, for example, where he comes in search of a job, he cannot square his inner feelings of "fear and emptiness" and his outward sense of something reduced in power: "he did not feel the pull and mystery of the thing [the wealthy neighborhood] as strongly as he had in the movie." We should recall that *Native Son* was published five years before the passage of the Ives-Quinn Act (1945), the first law forbidding discrimination in employment. Besides the personal conviction of helplessness that he has formed at home, there is a social stamp of hopelessness and uselessness for Bigger to bear. When in actuality he finds that the very neighborhood of the Daltons does not simply overpower him with the compounded weight of magical association and practical exaltation, that is to say, when he finds that he can keep walking, his mind makes a curious compensatory turn. He will be dangerous to "the white man" if the white man is not after all overwhelmingly dangerous to him. Bigger reacts to the loss of movie magic by investing himself with magical propensities: "he wanted to wave his hand and blot out the white man who was making him feel like this [afraid and worthless]. If not that, he wanted to blot himself out."

The fact is that Bigger blindly cultivates solitude at this point, desiring to be away from others or desiring others to be absent from him. This is the solitude of incapacity, which he must outgrow. The contrast with his final poised and poignant solitude in his jail cell is a measure of his growth in the novel. At that point, Bigger will exhibit a great but ineffectual capacity for communication, in the ambiguous condition of solitude that Wright enunciates in *The God That Failed*:

> Perhaps, I thought, out of my tortured feelings I could fling a spark into this darkness. I would try, not because I wanted to, but because I felt that I had to if I were to live at all.
>
> I would hurl words into this darkness and wait for an echo; and if an echo sounded, no matter how faintly, I would send other words to tell, to march, to fight, to create a sense of the hunger for life that gnaws in us all, to keep alive in our hearts a sense of the inexpressibly human.

In the early stages of *Native Son* Bigger Thomas needs as much to recover from a philosophical sense of magic as from a social and physical sense of terror and destruction. The further he goes into the latter, the more the former takes hold of his mind. He alternates between two complimentary states. First, he feels blithely secure, credulously falling asleep after the first killing, for example, and experiencing a "sense of fulness [that] he had so often but inadequately felt in magazines and movies." Second, he takes to feeling omnipotent, a condition expressed by various modulations of the following paradigm: "he wanted to wave his hand and blot them out." This magical gesture is addressed to his family, black people, Bessie, the world, his visitors in prison, the people at the inquest, "the sun's rising and setting." It is in the grip of this magic that he can be aggressively jubilant about having "killed a rich white girl and . . . burned her body . . . and . . . lied to throw the blame on someone else and . . . written a kidnap note demanding ten thousand dollars." We see a more realistic reaction when he is "afraid to touch food on the table, food which undoubtedly was his own." Tacitly, of course, the food-reluctance is related to an older magical belief that one fell into the power of those who gave one food. But in Bigger the fear of eating reveals a personal visceral distress and an unfocused, guilty feeling that others are secretly concocting harm for him.

The desire to sleep that overcomes Bigger when Mary's body is found and again after he takes Bessie's life represents the exhaustion of his sense of magic. His sense of reality will develop slowly, because it must be based on relationship and he is little versed in that. But the very idea of sleep grows complex for Bigger; rather than oblivion, it comes to mean peaceful courage and confidence and a religious sense "that all life was a sorrow that had to be accepted."

At this stage, the threat of annihilation no longer leads Bigger to homicidal defiance and magical self-inflation. In the novel's final section, "Fate," it is as though sleep has become metaphysical, and to rise from it a sort of resurrection. The language of resting "eternally" gives way to that of the rotted hull of a seed "forming the soil in which it should grow again." The dream of "a vast configuration of images and symbols whose magic and power could lift him up and make him live so intensely that the dread of being black . . . would be forgotten" gives way to a sense that "maybe the confused promptings, . . . the elation . . . were false lights that led nowhere." He can still resent being made a spectacle and a "sport" for others, especially white people, but he is now open to Jan Erlone in a way inconceivable before; and he is open to himself.

It is probably from Jan, with his comment that Bigger "believed [in himself] enough to kill," that Bigger takes the elements of his metaphysical self-proclamation; we may recall his anxious effort "to remember where he had heard words that would help him." His outcry flabbergasts his attorney, Boris Max: "I didn't want to kill . . . But what I killed for, *I am*! It must've been pretty deep in me." But this is after all a retrospective posture. More current is his desire for reconciliation, and the fact that "the impulsion to tell" the truth on which reconciliation must be based "was as deep as had been the urge to kill." The same kind of reversal of spirit appears in his desire to console and soothe his family, instead of defying and blotting them out.

And yet the last thing we see of Bigger precludes reconciliation; he is alone in his cell, smiling "a faint, wry, bitter smile," and hearing "the ring of steel against steel as a *far* door clanged shut" (emphasis mine). In effect the novel has brought him to personal, say even spiritual readiness for reconciliation, while removing him from the social context that makes reconciliation possible.

This paradox is lightened if we consider the question of Bigger's solitude. It is striking how often, throughout the story, Bigger finds or feels himself alone. Again and again we see him in the middle of a room or surrounded by others, in a state of presence without connection. From the outset, when his "gang" appears so prominent in his life, he is unconnected, and deliberately so, in that he cannot stand connection; it reminds him of his cowardice in the case of Gus and of his powerlessness in the case of his family. Bigger has thoughts of escaping the sense of solitude, but the escape takes the form of magic on the one hand and self-cancellation on the other:

> It was when he read the newspapers or magazines, or went to the movies, or walked along the streets with crowds, that he felt what he wanted: to merge himself with others and be a part of this world, to lose himself in it so he could find himself, to be allowed a chance to live like others, even though he was black.

But magical identification (magazines and movies) and social identification with others in the world stand in contrast in no more than superficial ways. Each entails a relapse into self-cancellation. Each is a desire for life as "a beautiful dream," for illusion, for unconsciousness. When the "cold white world" forces in on him, Bigger seeks another form of escape, by substitution: "If only someone had gone before and lived or suffered and died—made it so that it could be understood!" (He rejects Christianity, of course, though his language here conjures up Christ.) Again, he shuns his existential situation to join himself with another, in a passive, cheating unison—he wants it done and made easy for him, he wants to get out of going through it for himself.

It is striking that following his capture Bigger becomes his own Christological figure, coming back to himself after "three days" and "feeling . . . like the rotted hull of a seed forming in the soil in which it should grow again." The text is replete with (a) suggestions of original *and individual* creation ("some spirit had breathed and created him . . . in the image of a man with a man's obscure need and urge"); (b) images of individual growth ("a seed"); and (c) the language of singularity tempered but also confirmed by the force of the category ("he had to go forward and meet his end like any other living thing upon the earth"). To merge is impossible, but to belong ineluctable. Bigger has striven not to belong, adopting a mélange of materialism (note his retroactive effort to make money off Mary Dalton's killing), magical images, and self-cancelling postures. When he can face the mystery and the misery of being black and, more largely, of being human, he has shut himself off from its benefits by murder. The cry "what I killed for, I am!" causes Boris Max to flinch away, but that is not the cause of Bigger's being alone. The cause is in the act, and in the result of the act: "*I am!*" From self-cancellation Bigger has come to self-avowal, but through a passage with a cell at the end.

Bigger Thomas takes a place among the multitude of black protagonists who end up hiding away or running away or held away from some vital consummation. Needless to say, the line does not end with him; given that it is an expression of a cultural evolution, we should not expect it to. Earlier stages persist where new ones arise, and even interpenetrate with them. Captain Christian Laurent, in Ernest Gaines's "Bloodline," voluntarily isolates himself from a context in which *he has both purpose and power*, so that he represents an advanced capacity without an enlarged opportunity for black people. In the same vein, Nel finds herself "alone" at the end of Toni Morrison's *Sula*, alone and *looking back* at a lost opportunity for kinship with Sula and participation in the vision of freedom that Sula sought to embody. Bigger, as a preeminent figure in this line of grievous frustration, stands in the condition C. J. Rawson sees as the role adopted by Jean Genet, "homme et captif . . . , affirming his own solitude." But even in his solitude Bigger has something compelling and resonant for the future of black literature, the quality that frightens the same Boris Max who could take mere murder in stride, the ability to say to himself and to the echoing corridors of the society: "*I am!*"

Some difficulty may arise from the fact that Bigger Thomas remains essentially without connections, without amplitude. Ralph Ellison puts it tellingly in *Shadow and Act*:

> I . . . found it disturbing that Bigger Thomas had none of the finer qualities of Richard Wright, none of the imaginations, none of the sense of poetry, none of the gaiety. And I preferred Richard Wright to Bigger Thomas. Do you see? [This] . . . directs you back to the difference between what Wright was himself and . . . his conception of the quality of Negro humanity.

In Ellison's view, Wright took an overly "ideological" and deterministic position on the black condition. But it is worthwhile to ask what the essential tenet of Wright's ideology was, and whether at bottom, at least as regards Bigger Thomas, that ideology was sociopolitical or *metaphysical*. For Bigger goes through the naturalistic "fatalism" of the killings and the analytical "fatalism" of Boris Max's courtroom performance (to say nothing of the prosecutor's) into the self-discovery and implicit independence of his basic cry, "I am." In other words, while it would have been attractive to have a more autobiographical figure as protagonist, and a more cultivated personality in the manner of, say, Chester Himes's *The Primitive*, Wright would have paid a price for that. And the price would have had nothing to do with sociopolitical ideology. It would have fallen entirely in the metaphysical sphere, since Wright would have forgone any chance of showing a Bigger Thomas coming out of determinism into determination, out of rigid reaction into mobile being. The victim of "images" that we see in the early chapters emerges as a participant in a life of the spirit: "some spirit had breathed and created him . . . in the image of a man." Here image and identity fuse, so that he is free of illusion, even while the freedom of giving a certain substance to the image comes vainly into his hands.

The Tragic Hero

Joyce Anne Joyce

Bigger's predestined outcome, embodied in the elements of setting and the series of events that leads to his incarceration, illuminate him as the tragic hero. For he is alienated from both the black and white communities because of his volatile, stubborn, determined, prideful personality. This portrayal of Bigger challenges the stereotypical images of most black characters prior to 1940 and the traditional assumption that victimized characters and tragic heroes are mutually exclusive.

At the outset of his "Blueprint for Negro Writing," Wright addresses what he sees as the need of black writers to depict black characters that move beyond the limits of stereotypes and racial expectations:

> Generally speaking, Negro writing in the past has been confined to humble novels, poems, and plays, prim and decorous ambassadors who went a-begging to white America. They entered the Court of American Public Opinion dressed in the knee-pants of servility, curtsying to show that the Negro was not inferior, that he was human, and that he had a life comparable to that of other people. For the most part these artistic ambassadors were received as though they were French poodles who do clever tricks.

Ironically, this statement subtly undercuts the mistaken notion that Wright's depiction of Bigger Thomas is merely a plea for black

From *Richard Wright's Art of Tragedy.* © 1986 by the University of Iowa Press.

humanity and speaks to the need of black literature to represent truthfully the complicated consciousness of black Americans. With Bigger Thomas's psyche at its center, *Native Son* describes a young man who, when unaware of his emotional victimization, succumbs to the hysteria of racial oppression and who, after becoming conscious of his fears and emotional blindness, understands the role he has played in his suffering. Thus in his characterization of Bigger, Wright probes deep into human consciousness, revealing the intricacies of Bigger's personality that make him at once good and evil, fearful and defiant, awful and awesome.

This rendering of Bigger through these juxtapositions of opposites manifests itself in Wright's denunciation of the portrayals of blacks as simple one-dimensional figures. For Wright clearly understood that to depict black life in the midst of a vortex of social, political, and economic impediments does not demand that the depictions of black people be stereotypical or predominately reflections of victimization. An example of the dehumanizing effects of racial oppression and of the strength and ambiguity which the human spirit embodies, Bigger emerges as a rebellious, prideful, temperamental, challenging young hero whose suffering and emotional growth result from his refusal to acquiesce to the racial injustices of a Jim Crow society. The initial scenes of the novel make evident what becomes a most essential element of Bigger's personality: the interrelationship between his rebellious spirit and his strong sense of pride. Bigger's pride, which is apparent when we first meet him, undergirds the sullen indifference that typifies his interaction with his family and gang in book 1, motivates his rebelliousness in book 2, and awakens him at the beginning of book 3.

As the title of book 1 suggests, fear proves to be as strong an element of Bigger's personality as his pride. When confronted with the white world or with merely a suggestion of confrontation, Bigger most often becomes completely enwrapped by fear. This fear, which surfaces in Bigger's loss of control, is his *hamartia*, his mistake in judgment or the force responsible for his error in judgment. Throughout the novel, Bigger vacillates between indifference bolstered by his strong sense of pride and hysteria incited by his equally intense fear of the white world. Both immobility and fear engulf him as he accidentally murders Mary Dalton. Yet, despite this fear and the numerous opportunities he has to flee for his life before the discovery of Mary's bones, he defiantly remains among the Daltons, controlling and manipulating them through his awareness of the discrepancy between his reality and their illusions concerning that reality. The discovery that he is Mary's murderer results only from his loss of control—his inability to sustain a balance between fear and his new insight into the vulnerability of the white world. It is characteristic of tragedy that the same personality trait which accentuates the hero's humanness ironically precipitates his downfall—in this case Bigger's mistakes in judgment that lead to his murders, capture, and impending death.

Those passages in which Bigger's fear overwhelms his judgment and precipitates immobility, hysteria, or violence highlight the function of a third-person limited narrator who makes evident Bigger's thoughts, motives, and the subtle shifts in his consciousness. Since Wright's purpose is to present a work "so hard and deep that [his readers] would have to face it without the consolation of tears," his most difficult task is that of achieving an artistic balance between the aesthetic distance necessary to avoid excessive pity and empathy necessary to ensure the reader's admiration of Bigger's determination and spiritual awakening. The third-person point of view resolves this dilemma through its relationship with characterization. For Wright's central intelligence softens the impact of Bigger's volatile temperament and his tendency toward violence. Rather than illuminating a contradiction in Wright's intention to maintain an aesthetic distance, the third-person center of consciousness reflects instead the degree to which Wright—the tragic artist—commits himself to sustaining the tension throughout the thrust and parry of the ideas that embody Bigger's fate.

Susanne Langer's "The Tragic Rhythm" succinctly summarizes the movement of tragic drama, providing insight into the movement of *Native Son* as well as into the essence of Wright's depiction of Bigger:

> Tragic drama is so designed that the protagonist grows mentally, emotionally, or morally, by the demand of the action which he himself initiated, to the complete exhaustion of his powers, the limit of his possible development. He spends himself in the course of one dramatic action. This is, of course, a tremendous foreshortening of life; instead of undergoing the physical and psychical, many-sided, long process of an actual biography, the tragic hero lives and matures in some particular respect; his entire

being is concentrated in one aim, one passion, one conflict and ultimate defeat.

Wright, like the many tragedians before him, begins *Native Son* at a point in which the elements of his hero's past have already conspired to bring about Bigger's "ultimate defeat." The seeds of Bigger's destiny and his challenge of his fate are rooted in his obstinacy in taking the job at the Daltons'. Consequently, quite early in book 1, the job with the Daltons becomes the essential element of the dramatic action through which Bigger's characterization unfolds.

Bigger's resistance in accepting a job given to him by the relief office separates him emotionally from his family and friends as much as it does from the white world that provides the job. His aggressive slaughter of the huge rat, his dangling the rat in his sister's face, his habit of lying to his mother, and his routine fights with members of his gang exemplify his volatile temperament and rebelliousness long before he meets Mary Dalton. Distinctly different from the rest of his family and friends, Bigger is unable to acquiesce to the socioeconomic rules that govern the conditions in his home and in the rest of his community. His resentment of his family's stifled lives provokes his challenge of the Jim Crow codes that dominate their existence. His rebellious actions and pride consistently place him in opposition to the white world in a manner similar to that of the relationship between the Greeks and their gods: "To the Greeks, every action was a risk because it might invite the displeasure of a god; but, such was the tragic aspect of existence, man had to act. Great actions, the kind about which tragedies were written, involved great risks; and, since they inevitably involved a degree of *hubris,* they were ambiguous" (Richard B. Sewall, *The Vision of Tragedy*). Wright's descriptions of Bigger in the early scenes depict a young man whose proximity to whites is not only a risk to himself but also to those whites with whom he interacts. The explosive combination of Bigger's lack of exposure to whites, his rebelliousness, and his fear exacerbates the risks involved when he becomes employed in the Dalton home.

Bigger's actions reflect the ambiguity of his personality. The same pride that forces him to challenge the established order of things also bolsters his sullenness and the seeming indifference that hides his feelings. The narrator's descriptions of Bigger's thoughts after he upsets his entire family reveal the ambiguity in Bigger's character by highlighting the discrepancy between his awareness of the tenuous condition of his family and his response to this condition:

> He shut their voices out of his mind. He hated his family because he knew that they were suffering and that he was powerless to help them. He knew that the moment he allowed himself to feel to its fulness how they lived, the shame and misery of their lives, he would be swept out of himself with fear and despair. So he held toward them an attitude of iron reserve. . . . He denied himself and acted tough.

Suggesting the naturalness of Bigger's personality, Wright compares the aura of a flower that blooms mysteriously to the response Bigger's family and friends have toward his moods and sullen temperament. For his family and friends never know exactly how Bigger will respond to a given situation. His pride motivates him to action and sets him apart from the rest of the blacks in the novel. He hates and fears himself as he observes his behavior from a distance, but is unable to control himself because the hate and fear are so strong.

Bigger's accidental murder of Mary is an inevitable outcome of the socioeconomic elements of a Jim Crow society. However, his strong sense of pride and courageous spirit distinguish him significantly—tragically—from the typical naturalistic character. Sewall's description of Oedipus's *hubris* and the unfoldings of Oedipus's fate aptly applies to Bigger: "A man without *hubris* would have humbly acquiesced in his fate and let it unfold as it would. There would have been no significant action." Instead of humbly acquiescing, Bigger responds to Mary's death by taking control of his life and thrusting himself deeper into the tragic experience.

Emboldened by his own daring exploits in disposing of Mary's body and by his skillful manipulation of the Daltons and the police, Bigger challenges the stereotypical image of his blackness. Though Mary's murder, his framing Jan, his writing the kidnap note, and his implicating the Communist Party all attest to his rebelliousness, the courage he displays during the final scene of book 1, his capture, demonstrates his intensity, his "will to do or die, the uncompromising spirit which makes him pay any price, even life itself, for his object" (Henry A. Myers, *Tragedy: A View of Life*).

Wet and soiled from urinating in his clothes upon hitting the snow when he jumped out of the window of his room, hungry, almost frozen, frightened, and hysterically desperate for many hours, Bigger defiantly struggles to escape the hostile vigilantes. His reaction to the long awaited "There he is!" that signals his being spotted on the roof of a ramshackle building reflects a determination—characteristic of the tragic hero—to fight with every inch of his life: "The three words made him stop; he had been listening for them all night and when they came he seemed to feel the sky crashing soundlessly about him. What was the use of running? Would it not be better to stop, stand up, and lift his hands high above his head in surrender? Hell, naw! He continued to crawl."

It is no accident that the first person from Bigger's community to visit him in jail is Reverend Hammond. Just as most blacks in Bigger's community see themselves through the distorted images presented in the newspapers, they have also internalized the image of themselves as downtrodden, fated sufferers following the life of Christ. Thus Reverend Hammond's mission is to render Bigger submissive. Bigger, however, unlike his mother and the rest of his environment, rejects religion and its concomitant passivity and guilt. He is a man of action and necessity. For "he had killed within himself the preacher's haunting picture of life even before he had killed Mary; that had been his first murder."

Bigger has long intuitively recognized that the white world uses religion as a kind of sedative that minimizes rebelliousness in blacks. Bigger's adverse reaction to religion corresponds to what D. D. Raphael sees as the tragic hero's necessary defiance of religion: "Because Tragedy snatches a spiritual victory out of a natural defeat, it is nearer to the religious attitude than is Epic. In another way, however, Tragedy tends to be inimical to religion. It elevates man in his struggle with necessity, while the religious attitude is one of abasement before that which is greater than man, before the awe-inspiring sublime."

In addition to Bigger's rejection of religion, his murder of Bessie is another element of necessity which characterizes him as a tragic hero. His thoughts when he equates Bessie's alcohol with his mother's religion pinpoint his isolation from the rest of the community by emphasizing his will for the ideal—in this case social and economic retribution:

> He hated his mother for the way of hers which was like
> Bessie's. What his mother had was Bessie's whiskey, and
> Bessie's whiskey was his mother's religion. He did not

want to sit on a bench and sing, or lie in a corner and sleep. It was when he read the newspapers or magazines, went to the movies, or walked along the streets with crowds, that he felt what he wanted: to merge himself with others and be a part of this world, to lose himself in it so he could find himself, to be allowed a chance to live like others, even though he was black.

Ironically, Bigger's rebellious will to act in response to the socioeconomic restraints that preclude his being an integral part of American society further separates him from his family, friends, and the mainstream of American society.

Bessie's death clinches his rejection of the social norm of his environment. Her relationship to him and the feeling this relationship evokes in the reader call to mind Northrop Frye's description [in *Anatomy of Criticism*] of the female suppliant necessary to enhance the tragic mood. After discussing the *bomolochos*, or comic character that increases the comic mood, Frye continues:

The corresponding contrasting type in tragedy is the suppliant, the character, often female, who presents a picture of unmitigated helplessness and destitution. Such a figure is pathetic, and pathos, though it seems a gentler and more relaxed mood than tragedy, is even more terrifying. Its basis is the exclusion of an individual from a group, hence it attacks the deepest fear in ourselves that we possess. . . . In the figure of the suppliant pity and terror are brought to the highest possible pitch of intensity, and the awful consequences of rejecting the suppliant for all concerned is a central theme of Greek tragedy. Suppliant figures are often women threatened with death or rape.

Consequently, Bigger's rape and apparent superfluous murder of Bessie emerge as essential elements of Wright's tragic theme. Wright characterizes Bigger as the single individual who, through his preordained murder of Mary Dalton, is catapulted into taking control of his own life. The scene in which Bigger's mother, sister, brother, Jack, G.H., Gus, Buckley, Jan, Max, and the Daltons crowd around Bigger in a single room suggests that these characters are a kind of chorus "against which the hero's hybris may be measured" (Frye).

Bigger's *hubris* incites the defiance which underlies his strategy to remain in the Dalton home and to orchestrate the movement of his own destiny. He replaces his knife and gun, the previous symbols of his rebellion, with a new type of weapon—his awareness of the discrepancy between his reality and the white world's perception of him. This new insight stimulates Bigger's imagination and gives him self-confidence for the first time in his life. He assumes the role of the subversive strategist who comes to know his enemy far better than his enemy understands him. When questioned about Mary's absence by Mrs. Dalton, he quickly intuits the sociological and racist codes that prohibit Mrs. Dalton from searching below the surface of things: "he knew that a certain element of shame would keep Mrs. Dalton from asking him too much and letting him know that she was worried. He was a boy and she was an old woman. He was the hired and she was the hirer. . . . After all, he was black and she was white. He was poor and she was rich." And later when Bigger meets Britten, Mr. Dalton's private detective, Bigger effaces his intelligence, assuming a docile attitude that fulfills Britten's expectations. Bigger understands Britten on sight and slowly feeds him the information he wants him to have.

Chance affords Bigger a number of opportunities to attempt an escape long before his capture. Like the typical tragic hero, however, he plunges deeper into the tragic experience, choosing not only to fight, but also to shape his destiny. As he carries Mary's trunk to the car in his perfunctory move of taking it to the train station, he contemplates leaving with the money he had taken from Mary's purse. But self-confidence and excitement motivate his decision to test his will to its extreme. And even after Britten's hostile, intense interrogation, Bigger gathers his defiant forces, determined to outwit his adversaries:

> Bigger went to the window and looked out at the white curtain of falling snow. He thought of the kidnap note. Should he try to get money from them now? Hell, yes! He would show that Britten bastard! . . . He'd give that Britten something to worry about, all right. Just wait.
>
> Because he could go now, run off if he wanted to and leave it all behind, he felt a certain sense of power, a power born of a latent capacity to live.

The series of events that unfolds once Bigger reaches the Dalton home gives him the opportunity to take the risk which pushes to the surface his hidden potential to pursue life to its fullest, to push himself in order to discover his greatest possibilities. By showing Bigger's rebellious nature, which has always isolated him from the black community and branded him a threat to the white community, Wright depicts Bigger as the hero whose desires exceed the limitations peculiar to a Jim Crow society.

No matter how well planned, Bigger's crafty strategy is destined for failure. The success of his choice of action depends upon his ability to control his fear, and ironically it is this fear which causes him to lose control and thus precipitates his capture. Although malevolent external forces play an essential role in setting the tragic pattern in motion, Bigger's psychological makeup is responsible for the errors in judgment that produce and sustain the tragic action. In the initial scenes, Bigger's sullen treatment of his family and the violent display of emotions that instigates the fight with Gus spring from his fear. In the case of his family, Bigger assumes a sullen persona because he fears the vulnerability of love and responsibility.

Quite simply, he fights with Gus because he fears whites intensely. In describing Bigger's feelings as he waits for Gus to agree to rob their first white store-owner, the narrator explains how Bigger transfers his fear of whites to violence toward Gus:

> He hated Gus because he knew that Gus was afraid, as even he was; and he feared Gus because he felt that Gus would consent and then he would be compelled to go through with the robbery. . . . He watched Gus and waited for him to say yes. . . . Then he could not stand it any longer. The hysterical tensity of his nerves urged him to speak, to free himself. He faced Gus, his eyes red with anger and fear, his fists clenched and held stiffly to his sides.

The contradiction between Bigger's fear of robbing a white man and the fact that he himself is the originator of the idea to rob Blum reflects the irreconcilable aspects of his personality. He vacillates between fear and hate, hate and shame, sullenness and hysteria.

Just as his loss of control with Gus alienates him completely from his gang, the hysteria which overcomes him when Mrs. Dalton enters Mary's room brings about Mary's death. Bigger's fear of whites, and their lack of perception of how environmental forces have shaped their psyches quite differently from his, function conjointly to presage Bigger's murder of Mary. The scenes that portray Bigger's contempt for Mary as she naively questions him about unions and communism, and his extreme discomfort with Jan and Mary in Ernie's Kitchen Shack, all stimulate in Bigger a desire to "leap" to action to destroy the emotions that overwhelm him. Wright's frequent use of the word *leap* in describing Bigger when he feels most entrapped and the imagery that compares Bigger's feelings to the processes of nature suggest that Bigger reacts instinctively when confronted with a representative of the world that seeks to dominate him.

Bigger understands that being in Mary Dalton's room automatically means that he has broken the most important law of the cosmological order characteristic of a Jim Crow society. Consequently, when blind Mrs. Dalton enters Mary's room, Bigger completely loses control as his fear powerfully overwhelms him. When Mrs. Dalton approaches the bed, he becomes caught up in a spell of hysteria, intuitively acting to safe his life. Throughout this scene that moves very quickly, Wright charts Bigger's reactions so vividly that a careful reading of the scene precludes any idea that Bigger acts with evil intent. As Mary tries to rise from the bed in response to her mother's voice,

> *Frenzy* dominated him. He held his hand over her mouth and his head was cocked at an angle that enabled him to see Mary and Mrs. Dalton by merely shifting his eyes. Mary mumbled and tried to rise again. *Frantically* he caught a corner of the pillow and brought it to her lips. He had to stop her from mumbling, or he would be caught. Mrs. Dalton was moving slowly toward him and he grew tight and full, as though about to explode. Mary's fingernails tore at his hands and he caught the pillow and covered her entire face with it firmly. . . .
>
> His eyes were filled with the white blur moving toward him in the shadows of the room. Again Mary's body heaved and he held the pillow in a grip that took all of his strength. . . .
>
> He clenched his teeth and held his breath, intimidated to the core by the awesome white blur floating toward him. His muscles flexed taut as steel and he pressed the pillow, feeling the bed give slowly, evenly, but silently. (emphasis mine)

One of the most important scenes in the novel, this necessarily long passage demonstrates the intensity of Bigger's fear and shows the extent to which fear holds him in a trance, causing him literally to lose sight of everything around him, except the "white blur."

Ironically, then, Bigger's act of carrying Mary to her room to save himself from blame and harm backfires cataclysmically. Of more importance, and equally ironic, is the fact that the failure of his attempts to defy his destiny is in part rooted in his own psyche. As long as he maintains his self-control, he is able to sustain the emotional stability and strength he needs to meet any sudden, unexpected change. Any arousal of fear renders him vulnerable and ineffectual. The furnace, which continually excites his fear to an intensity comparable to that responsible for his murder of Mary, is the curse or mistake that instigates Bigger's capture. Like his fear of whites, fear of the furnace rhythmically presages danger and entrapment. When he carries Mary's body to the basement, he intends to dispose of her by using the trunk until he spontaneously decides to burn her in the furnace. His burning Mary compounds the levels of irony that lead to his incarceration. For both his fear of the furnace and the lingering images of Mary's body haunt him and finally cause him to become so immobilized that he pinpoints himself as her murderer.

His crucial mistake in judgment is his delay in cleaning the furnace. Because of his intense fear of attracting attention to the furnace, he permits the coal to pile up, knowing that the ashes could eventually block the air ducts:

> He stood a moment looking through the cracks into the humming fire, blinding red now. But how long would it keep that way, if he did not shake the ashes down? He remembered the last time he had tried and how hysterical he had felt. . . . He imagined that if he shook it he would see pieces of bone falling into the bin and he knew that he would not be able to endure it. He jerked upright and, lashed by fiery whips of fear and guilt, backed hurriedly to the door. . . . He could not bring himself to shake those ashes.

Bigger continues to stall, hoping that the reporters and Britten will leave the house. Instead of leaving, the reporters, excited by the coverage of Mary's absence in their daily papers, decide to question Bigger again and to take pictures of him and the Daltons. When it gets cool in the house, the moment finally arrives when Peggy, as she brings coffee to the reporters, asks Bigger to clean the ashes.

Her request confounds Bigger as much as the shepherd's story of Oedipus's past befuddles Oedipus. Bigger's first thoughts reveal his emotions: "Clean the fire out! Good God! Not now, not with the men standing round." The movements that follow progress as quickly and as intensely as those of the rat scene. Bigger gradually loses control. Against all his will, he knows he has to respond to Peggy's order because the other whites have heard her. He opens the door to the storage bin and decides to add more coal, hoping that the fire will burn until the basement is free of the reporters. On the contrary, the smoke burgeons rapidly, choking him, filling the room, and stifling the reporters. When a reporter frantically takes the shovel, Bigger knows that he no longer has control of the situation: "He wanted to go to him and ask for the shovel; he wanted to say that he could take care of it now. But he did not move. He felt that he had let things slip through his hands to such an extent that he could not get at them again." When the reporter with the shovel stares incredulously into the ashes, Bigger's worst fear materializes. Wright compares Bigger's feelings to the malfunctioning of the furnace, suggesting the symbolic relationship between Bigger's fear and the furnace: "Bigger edged forward, his lungs not taking in or letting out air; he himself was a huge furnace now through which no air could go; and the fear that surged into his stomach, filling him, choking him, was like the fumes of smoke that had belched from the ash bin." Overwhelmed by the fear responsible for his error in judgment, Bigger again attempts to defy his destiny. While the reporters are entranced by what they find in the ashes, Bigger escapes.

Although we do not sanction his murder of Mary, we empathize with him because of the intense fear that motivates his actions. Thus, characteristic of tragedy, Bigger's *hamartia*—his loss of control caused by fear—plays the paradoxical role of making him at once vulnerably human and threateningly awesome. Despite our knowing that Bigger's fate and our moral code demand that he be captured, we become involved in his struggle to evade the vigilantes. For Wright's adroit use of a third-person limited narrator controls the degree to which we identify with Bigger's tragedy. Katherine Fishburn summarizes the function of the narrator in *Native Son*: "*Native Son* is told entirely from the viewpoint of Bigger Thomas, the narrator; we never know what is in the minds of other characters. In limiting himself to Bigger's perspective, Wright is asking the reader to identify with his hero and to try to understand his motives and actions." The role of the narrator is to soften the reader's harsh judgment of Bigger by establishing an affinity between the reader's consciousness and Bigger's, and thus ensuring that we feel Bigger's fate as our own. The tragic artist traditionally creates a hero whose courage and defiance incite our admiration and censure. We censure the hero when his actions offend our sensibilities and separate us from him, and we admire him—from a sublime distance—as he fights in the face of all adversity.

Although the narrator identifies completely with Bigger, as Fishburn explains, he is not to be confused with Bigger. Because Bigger is inarticulate and incommunicative throughout most of the novel, the narrator reveals the seething world of Bigger's psyche, illuminating motives and thoughts Bigger fails to perceive. Vacillating between extreme sullenness and an explosive temper, Bigger lacks the introspection that brings self-knowledge. The narrator "at the most crucial points of action and self-recognition, becomes a sort of translator, or refiner, of the stifled, muddled intensity of Bigger's inner life" (Larsen). With the exception of Bigger's murder of Mary, the essential action in *Native Son* takes place in Bigger's mind. This internal counteraction functions—by means of the narrator—as an element of the tragic dialectic through which the effects of Bigger's suffering unfold.

An informed, keen, and sensitive narrator provides the comprehensive look at Bigger's thoughts, revealing the reasons for the sullen moods, iron reserve, volatile temperament, and fear which characterize Bigger in book 1. After Bigger kills Mary, the narrator, throughout book 2, intermittently directs attention to the emotional battle that takes place in Bigger's mind. At the same time that he struggles defiantly to forge his own destiny by outwitting the Daltons and the police, Bigger fights a battle to overcome the guilt and stress that persistently threaten him. While his fear of the furnace is the final cause of his loss of control, the haunting image of Mary's bloody head also works to subdue him. Complementing the narrator's explanation of Bigger's motives, the references to the lingering images of Mary's body help to counterbalance the portrayal of Bigger's violent nature and thus mitigate against the reader's harsh judgment of him.

Working against the strength that manifests itself when Bigger faces the Daltons and Britten, the images of Mary's head become opposing internal forces that reflect the divisive personality characteristic of the tragic hero. These recurring images highlight the seething emotional turbulence hidden by Bigger's mask of composure. When he approaches the furnace and imagines that he sees Mary's head, he risks losing his mask:

> The inside of the furnace breathed and quivered in the grip of fiery coals. But there was no sign of the body, even though the body's image hovered before his eyes, between his eyes and the bed of coals burning hotly. . . .
>
> At the moment he stooped to grasp the protruding handle of the lower bin to shake it to and fro, a vivid image of Mary's face as he had seen it upon the bed in the blue light of the room gleamed at him from the smoldering embers and he rose abruptly, giddy and hysterical with guilt and fear. His hands twitched.

This picture of Bigger's vulnerability serves the same functions as the narrator's description of the fear and mixed emotions Bigger experiences in his home and with his gang. Outwardly tough and intractable in his attitude toward his family and friends, and manipulative and shrewd in his treatment of the Daltons and the police, Bigger is always inwardly quite fearful and neurotic.

The relationship between the image of Mary's head and Bigger's increasing anxiety reaches its peak in a bizarre dream which discloses the depth of Bigger's apprehensions. After Britten initially interrogates him, Bigger, physically and emotionally exhausted, slips into a deep sleep in which he dreams he hears a ringing church bell that grows louder as he stands on a street corner. He stands in a red glare like the glare from the furnace, holding a heavy, wet, and slippery package. When he unwraps the package, he discovers his own head with wet bloody hair. When white people begin to close in on him asking questions about the head, he awakes slowly, realizing that the sound is coming from the doorbell of his room. From the moment the bell begins to ring directly over Bigger's head Wright describes how Bigger's waking fears reflect his unconsciousness. The approximately 316 unpunctuated words of Bigger's dream diminish the emotional barriers between Bigger's unconscious mind and our own.

Wright achieves a skillful balance between those elements which evoke the reader's identification with Bigger and those that detach us from him. The narrator's astute translations of Bigger's thoughts as well as the numerous descriptions of Bigger's emotional and physical fatigue counteract our response to the repugnant scenes in which Bigger chops off Mary's head with the hatchet and batters Bessie's face with a brick. Even Bigger's daring, hardened attempts to carry out his scheme of collecting money by using the kidnap note are accompanied by the narrator's intermittent descriptions of Bigger's nervousness and extreme exhaustion. When Bessie deduces why Bigger is certain that Mary will not show up to thwart his plans of collecting the kidnap money, the narrator calls attention to the change Bessie's recognition of Bigger as a murderer effects in him:

> His jaw clamped tight and he stood up. . . . He began to feel cold; he discovered that his body was covered with sweat. He heard a soft rustle and looked down at his hand; the kidnap note was shaking in his trembling fingers. But I ain't scared, he told himself. He folded the note, put it into an envelope, sealed it by licking the flap, and shoved it in his pocket.

Hence despite his fear, exhaustion, and the odds against him, Bigger is a man driven by the necessity to test his power.

In fact, Bigger's will is so strong that we tend to overlook the implications inherent in the narrator's descriptions of Bigger's struggle to avoid collapsing. After Bigger slips the kidnap note under the Daltons' door and burns the gloves and pencil and paper, physical weakness, fear, and anxiety sap his strength, illuminating his loneliness and agonizing sense of guilt:

> A strange sensation enveloped him. Something tingled in his stomach and on his scalp. His knees wobbled, giving way. He stumbled to the wall and leaned against it weakly. A wave of numbness spread fanwise from his stomach over his entire body, including his head and eyes, making his mouth gap. Strength ebbed from him. He sank to his knees and pressed his fingers to the floor to keep from tumbling over. An organic sense of dread seized him. His teeth chattered and he felt sweat sliding down his armpits and back. He groaned, holding as still as possible. His vision was blurred; but gradually it cleared. Again he saw the furnace. Then he realized that he had been on the verge of collapse.

Bigger's exhaustion and loneliness grow as he fights for his freedom.

With Bessie, before her death, as his only marginal companion, he is enwrapped by an "organic sense of dread" and is unable to sleep and eat.

He runs to Bessie not only for the money from Mary's purse, but also because he yearns for companionship. Thus his initial thoughts are not of murder. But while he is in Bessie's presence, her cowering makes him see that including her in his plans has been a mistake. His realization of the necessity to kill Bessie comes to him suddenly and firmly from the depths of consciousness: "He wondered if she was sleeping; somewhere deep in him he knew that he was lying there waiting for her to go to sleep. Bessie did not figure in what was before him." He fidgets with the brick, the flashlight, and the blanket, delaying the act that he himself finds totally repugnant. The narrator carefully explains that Bigger's heart beats wildly, his breath swells, and his muscles flex as he tries "to impose his will over his body." Only his thoughts of Mary's burning body, of Britten, and of the law help him overcome his revulsion at the idea of killing Bessie.

After Bessie's death, Bigger flees through and across the tops of apartment buildings, trying to evade capture. Throughout these scenes that lead to Bigger's incarceration, the narrator persistently points to Bigger's isolation and loneliness and describes the effects of his hunger and of the cold, icy water from the fire hose that finally whirls him onto his back. Still functioning as an essential means of sustaining a balance between the opposing aspects of Bigger's personality, the narrator at the beginning of book 3 becomes obtrusive because Bigger is in a semiconscious state and because he grapples with ideas completely new to him. And near the end of the novel, the narrator virtually disappears when Bigger, stimulated by Max's questions that plunge him deep into introspection and retrospection, begins to articulate his own feelings. The articulate, pensive, tranquil Bigger who emerges from book 3 is quite different from the sullen, temperamental, neurotic young man who reports to work at the Dalton home. Bigger's suffering yields knowledge and is responsible for the change in character Sewell holds necessary to tragedy: "One simple criterion of tragedy lies in the question, How does our first view of the protagonist . . . differ from what we see at the end? Has there been a gain, if only minimal, in humanity, self-knowledge, wisdom, insight—all that we have subsumed under the notion of perception?"

The price that Bigger must pay for his new knowledge of self is suffering and death. The change that he undergoes begins, of course, when he takes the job at the Daltons' and continues as he struggles to escape the police. His incarceration in book 3 enhances his suffering and catapults him into a vortex of new emotions that lead to his discovery of self-awareness. Pride forces him to attempt again to control his own life. Traditionally, pride is the tragic flaw that makes the hero vulnerable to the forces that attempt to subdue him and ironically precipitates his transcendence.

The inquest scene which opens book 3 brings Bigger closer to his fate. Having failed in his attempt to bring meaning into his life, he yearns to reach inside himself to destroy that which gave him hope. His coma symbolizes his "deep physiological resolution not to react to anything." Because Bigger is only semiconscious and because his confinement brings him into the realm of completely new experiences, the narrator plays a key role in interpreting Bigger's feelings. He even goes so far as to explain that Bigger cannot intellectualize his feelings of renunciation; instead, "this feeling sprang up of itself, organically, automatically; like the rotted hull of a seed forming the soil in which it should grow again."

Bigger's organic desire to pull completely inward, to kill himself, is as instinctive as the indignation that forces him to consciousness when he perceives that the purpose of the inquest is to mock and demean him. The narrator describes Bigger's movement toward consciousness and rebellion as he watches those around him in the large room of the Cook County Morgue:

> There was in the air a silent mockery that challenged him. It was not their hate he felt; it was something deeper than that. He sensed that in their attitude toward him they had gone beyond hate. . . . Though he could not put it into words, he felt that not only had they resolved to put him to death, but that they were determined to make his death mean more than a mere punishment. . . . And as he felt it, rebellion rose in him. He had sunk to the lowest point this side of death, but when he felt his life again threatened in a way that meant that he was to go down the dark road a helpless spectacle of sport for others, he sprang back into action, alive, contending.

The same rebellious attitude and pride that characterize Bigger in books 1 and 2 spring him back to consciousness with a new determination to defy the powerful, capricious forces that challenge his self-respect.

This time his pride forces him to do battle in an emotional arena rather than a physical one. During the course of his confinement, his consciousness grows in depth and perceptivity. Although Bigger's initial response to Max does not differ significantly from his reaction to Buckley or any of the whites around him, he eventually responds to Max's questions, which are designed to extract from him the reasons for the drives and fears that made him react so intensely as to kill. When Bigger first feels the urge to talk, his inexperience at self-evaluation thwarts him:

> Bigger was staring straight before him, his eyes wide and shining. His talking to Max had evoked again in him that urge to talk, to tell, to try to make his feelings known. A wave of excitement flooded him. He felt that he ought to be able to reach out with his bare hands and carve from naked space the concrete, solid reasons why he had murdered. He felt them that strongly. If he could do that, he would relax; he would sit and wait until they told him to walk to the chair; and he would walk.

This passage punctuates Bigger's emerging need to establish some link between himself and the rest of humanity and his desire to discover, for the first time in his life, who he is so that he might die with dignity.

His drive to communicate places him inside the world. Lying on his cot and reflecting upon the events of his life, he begins to understand that he has never been as unconnected to others as he had thought. After his family visits him in jail and relates the black and white communities' maltreatment of them in response to Bigger's crimes, he realizes that his life indeed affects the well-being of his family. This discovery of a link with something outside himself, along with Max's subsequent questions, unleashes thoughts and feelings that had been unfamiliar to Bigger. Explaining Bigger's thoughts after a long session with Max, the narrator reveals Bigger's trepidation at the new thoughts forming within him:

> For the first time in his life he had gained a pinnacle of

feeling upon which he could stand and see vague relations that he had never dreamed of. If that white looming mountain of hate were not a mountain at all, but people, people like himself, and like Jan—then he was faced with a high hope the like of which he had never thought could be, and a despair the full depths of which he knew he could not stand to feel.

Bigger, however, is not able "to leave this newly seen and newly felt thing alone."

The entire experience of the trial and the physical limitations that confinement places upon Bigger thrust him even deeper into self-analysis. Although he does not comprehend the words in Max's speech, the mere act of the speech and Max's seeming sincerity move Bigger to want "to talk with him and feel with as much keenness as possible what his living and dying meant." During this last scene in which both Bigger and Max face each other with the knowledge that the governor has refused Bigger's appeal, Bigger's self-revelation reveals the outcome of the long emotional battle that has characterized him in book 3.

In a long and powerful speech that demonstrates Bigger's growth and makes it clear that a subtle change has taken place in the relationship between him and the narrator, the new Bigger evinces that his suffering has yielded the knowledge of his affinity with the rest of mankind:

"Mr. Max, I sort of saw myself after that night. And I sort of saw other people, too." Bigger's voice died; he was listening to the echoes of his words in his own mind. He saw amazement and horror on Max's face. Bigger knew that Max would rather not have him talk like this; but he could not help it. He had to die and he had to talk. "Well, it's sort of funny, Mr. Max. I ain't trying to dodge what's coming to me." Bigger was growing hysterical. "I know I'm going to get it. I'm going to die. Well, that's all right now. But really I never wanted to hurt nobody. That's the truth, Mr. Max. I hurt folks 'cause I felt I had to; that's all. They were crowding me too close; they wouldn't give me no room. Lots of times I tried to forget 'em, but I couldn't. They wouldn't let me. . . ." Bigger's eyes were wide and unseeing; his voice rushed on; "Mr. Max I didn't mean to do what I did. I was trying to do something else. But it seems like I never could. I was always wanting something and I was feeling that nobody would let me have it. So I fought 'em. I thought they was hard and I acted hard." He paused, then whimpered in confession, "But I ain't hard, Mr. Max. I ain't hard even a little bit. . . ." He rose to his feet. "But I—I won't be crying none when they take me to that chair. But I'll b-b-be feeling inside of me like I was crying. . . . I'll be feeling and thinking that they didn't see me and I didn't see them. . . ."

Bigger understands and articulates quite coherently what he is and how he became what he is. Bigger's spiritual awakening now complete, we no longer need the narrator to intermediate, to bridge the gap between Bigger's turbulent consciousness and our perception of that consciousness. The rebelliousness, the pride, the volatile temperament, and the fear are superseded by a new depth that embodies self-knowledge and spiritual growth.

Having found hope within himself, Bigger takes emotional responsibility for himself, forcing his reality upon the worn and resigned Max. Moreover, the narrator, who previously guided the reader through the flux and flow of Bigger's consciousness in books 1 and 2, and the initial parts of book 3, becomes less obtrusive. Wright interweaves dramatic dialogue with the interpretive voice of the narrator to accentuate Bigger's ability to express the depths of his own thoughts. The reader, then, is able to separate Bigger's consciousness from the voice of the narrator. Instead of serving their usual role as translators of Bigger's thoughts, the narrator's comments function as asides or stage directions. From this point on, the narrator virtually disappears and the novel progresses to its end through dramatic dialogue between Max and Bigger.

Bigger emerges from his ordeal as a composite, individual personality whose tragic fate arouses our compassion as well as our alarm. We do not forget that while external forces always set the tragic pattern into action, the hero himself is in part responsible for his fate. Bigger, too, realizes this as his "faint, wry, bitter smile" follows Max down the steel corridors when Max leaves him to his impending death. This understanding of his role in his fate and of the emotional liaison that binds all of humanity make Bigger a universal hero, pulling him out of the mire of naturalism into the realm of tragedy.

Through the magnitude of his suffering and through his perception of it, Bigger joins a host of protagonists whose suffering Sewall cites as tragic. In reference to the protagonists of *The Scarlet Letter, Moby-Dick,* and *The Brothers Karamazov,* Sewall writes, "That these people achieve tragic stature—anything but 'little'—is due in large part to their capacities, developed through suffering, to understand themselves, judge themselves, and see in their lot an image of the universal."

The Dissociated Sensibility of Bigger Thomas

Louis Tremaine

Native Son is offensive to most readers of taste. Even critics sympathetic to Richard Wright's 1940 novel have generally stressed its historical and sociological importance while deploring many of its "literary failings." And the offense has nothing to do with the "postmodernist" violence that has been done to fiction (or to the reader's expectations of it). Wright's book, rather, is an assault "from below." Its characters (apart from Bigger Thomas) are painfully transparent stereotypes; the plot is uniformly extravagant and improbable; the narrative perspective awkwardly straddles a gulf between the consciousness of an uneducated and unreflective protagonist and a third-person narrator who often conveys his character's motivation in the abstract jargon of a social scientist. In the last ten years, a flurry of studies have appeared defending (successfully for the most part) the composition of the final section of the novel with its lengthy, "propagandistic" courtroom oration by Bigger's lawyer. But while these studies have restored a certain balance to the critical discussion of the work, they have done so at the cost of a piecemeal approach to the text.

It is time to put *Native Son* together again. What is most characteristic of the text, from first to last, and which therefore cannot be ignored, is precisely that which "offends" the reader's expectations

From *Studies in American Fiction* 14, no. 1 (Spring 1986). © 1986 by Northeastern University.

of it as a serious work of fiction. By looking at, rather than away from, Wright's handling of character, plot, and narration, one discovers that these elements point directly to a dissociated sensibility lying at the heart of Bigger Thomas. They are, in fact, the effective means by which the book as a whole functions as a formal projection of Bigger's struggle toward self-expression.

A number of critics have observed already that there exists a "split consciousness" in Bigger and have analyzed the various ethical and perceptual conflicts that plague him. What needs further attention in order to understand the kind of dissociation that Bigger suffers, however, is the specific consequences of these conflicts for the character. In *Native Son*, these consequences are described repeatedly and forcefully and constitute a highly consistent pattern. Bigger's essential dilemma is not simply his ethical hesitation between social values and self-interest, not simply his perceptual confusion of concrete reality and abstract symbol, but his inability, in his daily functioning, to express his emotional experience in ways that make its meaning accessible both to his own consciousness and to the consciousness of those around him. It is this dissociated sensibility, this conflict between experience and expression where there should be complementarity, that makes of Bigger a mass of unsatisfied urges, that creates "the rhythms of his life: indifference and violence," that defines Bigger's very existence:

> There was something he *knew* and something he *felt*; something the *world* gave him and something he *himself* had; something spread out in *front* of him and something spread out in *back*; and never in all his life, with this black skin of his, had the two worlds, thought and feeling, will and mind, aspiration and satisfaction, been together; never had he felt a sense of wholeness.

It is his longing somehow to bring these dissociated parts of himself together and thereby "explain" himself, create a true image of his feelings, that causes him to cling so desperately to life though condemned to certain death:

> He felt that he ought to be able to reach out with his bare hands and carve from naked space the concrete, solid reasons why he had murdered. He felt them that strongly. If

he could do that, he would relax; he would sit and wait until they told him to walk to the chair; and he would walk.

This hunger for self-expression is due in part to socioeconomic conditions that deny Bigger access to conventional modes of communication, to the tools of language and culture systematically reserved for the use of the dominant race and class. This is clear to most readers and is made explicit in Max's courtroom speech. But what Wright is most concerned with is the ways in which an individual's experience is distorted by these conditions. It is true that Bigger lacks words, audience, and forum, but the primary reason for his failure of self-expression is his fear of what he has to express, a characteristic and generalized fear that repeatedly blocks any efforts to integrate his own sensibility.

Partially responsible, of course, is a fear of whites, which not only motivates his fight with Gus but prevents him from understanding the nature of that motivation:

> His confused emotions had made him feel instinctively that it would be better to fight Gus than to confront a white man with a gun. But he kept this knowledge of his fear thrust firmly down in him; his courage to live depended upon how successfully his fear was hidden from his consciousness.

But the willful suppression of awareness described in this passage operates in many other areas of his life as well and accounts for the imagery of barriers (walls, curtains, veils, and related images) which is so often commented on by critics. The first time such imagery appears is in the context of Bigger's efforts to shield himself from the wretched conditions of his existence and, more importantly, from his fear of *himself* as he faces those conditions:

> He hated his family because he knew that they were suffering and that he was powerless to help them. He knew that the moment he allowed himself to feel to its fullness how they lived, the shame and misery of their lives, he would be swept out of himself with fear and despair. So . . . he lived with them, but behind a wall, a curtain. . . . He knew that the moment he allowed what his life

meant to enter fully into his consciousness, he would either kill himself or someone else.

A similar failure—or refusal—to delve into his own experience affects the operation of Bigger's consciousness with respect to religion as he knows it, to his marginal legal status, to the threat of betrayal in human relationships, and to other areas of Bigger's fear-ridden life from which he seeks instinctively to protect himself. Such situations are repeatedly presented in language that emphasizes this process of suppression: "Not once . . . had an image of what he had done come into his mind. He had thrust the whole thing back of him"; "there appeared before him . . . images which in turn aroused impulses long dormant, impulses that he had suppressed and sought to shunt from his life"; "A strong counter-emotion waxed in him, warning him to leave this newly seen and newly felt thing alone." Bigger is thus caught between his deep need to make his own experience manifest to himself and his equally deep fear of doing so.

Bigger, in fact, yearns to make himself understood not only to himself but to those with whom he shares the world. He fears, however, that any attempt to establish such an understanding is futile and will only confirm his sense that he is different—different not only as a black but as Bigger. This longing for connectedness is at times directed toward "his people" (a term he fails to understand when it is spoken to him by the Daltons), "but that dream would fade when he looked at the other black people near him. Even though black like them, he felt there was too much difference between him and them to allow for a common binding and a common life." Later, as he awaits trial and execution, the yearning becomes more generalized:

> And if he reached out with his hands and touched other people, . . . if he did that would there be a reply, a shock? . . . And in that touch, response of recognition, there would be union, identity; there would be a supporting oneness, a wholeness which had been denied him all his life.

Such desires, though buried deep, are strong in Bigger and rise up confusingly as a result of his encounters with Mary, Jan, and Max, as well as of the existential crisis he faces as a condemned man.

His need is to communicate, and yet his instinct, an instinct he overcomes only with Max, is to dissemble. This becomes a recurring motif in Bigger's interactions with others throughout the book: he gauges how he is perceived, calculates what is expected of him, and then acts (in both senses of the word) to direct attention away from himself as he is and toward a more desirable image of himself. His fight with Gus, for example, is an effort to hide his fearful and irresolute nature from his poolroom friends and from Doc. He puts on a different sort of act for Mr. Dalton:

> He stood with his knees slightly bent, his lips partly open, his shoulders stooped; and his eyes held a look that went only to the surface of things. There was an organic conviction in him that this was the way white folks wanted him to be in their presence.

With Peggy, he adjusts his table manners and tries to express the sympathy for the Daltons that he thinks she expects of him. He "distrusts" and "hates" Jan and Mary because he cannot read their expectations and act accordingly. After the first murder, he is concerned with maintaining a pretense of normalcy with his mother: "He knew at once that he should not have acted frightened"; "He felt that his acting in this manner was a mistake"; "He had spoken in the wrong tone of voice; he had to be careful." With Britten, he stands "with sleepy eyes and parted lips," even while hating him enough to want to kill him. There is, in fact, no character in the book whose relations with Bigger are not explicitly conditioned by this need of Bigger's to mask his true feelings. Even with Max, he is initially wary and gradually makes his first ineffectual attempts to express himself to another only in response to a concerted—and professional—effort on Max's part to elicit Bigger's confidence. Max's repeated question "How do you feel, Bigger?" is no mere formulaic greeting.

Bigger yearns to understand his own feelings by expressing them both to himself and to others, but his fear both of himself and of others is an obstacle to such expression. Still, it might be asked whether he would be capable of such expression even if this barrier were removed. Certainly he lacks verbal talent and training. Bigger *is*, however, an image-maker. This particular expressive faculty comes into play at least three times in the novel and in all three cases is released under the impetus of strong sensation. The first two of these occur during the sexual act:

> He floated on a wild tide, rising and sinking with the ebb and flow of her blood, being willingly dragged into a warm

night sea to rise renewed to the surface to face a world he hated and wanted to blot out of existence, clinging close to a fountain whose warm waters washed and cleaned his senses.

He galloped a frenzied horse down a steep hill in the face of a resisting wind. . . . And then the wind became so strong that it lifted him high into the dark air, turning him, twisting him, hurling him.

The third and most significant instance of extended mental image-making occurs in Bigger's cell, as he is "tired, sleepy, and feverish" but feels a "war raging in him." The narrator is explicit here about Bigger's struggle to integrate his sensibility. "Blind impulses welled up in his body, and his intelligence sought to make them plain to his understanding by supplying images that would explain them." Elaborate images of a "black sprawling prison" and a "strong blinding sun" follow, expressing hate and fear and a longing for wholeness respectively. It is at these rare moments in the book that Bigger is most at one with himself, that his feelings are most fully present to his consciousness.

His need remains, however, to externalize and project these feelings, either through direct communication or through other expressive behavior. A considerable case is made in the novel, and accepted by many critics, for the murder of Mary as Bigger's one successful expressive act. He insists to himself that the crime was no accident, that he "had killed many times before, only on those other times there had been no handy victim or circumstance to make visible or dramatic his will to kill," that in this act the "hidden meaning of his life . . . had spilled out." Even Max, in court, refers to the need of black people for self-expression and then characterizes Bigger's crime as "an act of creation." These remarks concern the killing of Mary in particular, but she and Bessie and the rat in Bigger's apartment are merely the most obvious, not the only, murder victims portrayed in the book. For in his mind, Bigger actively fantasizes killing Gus, Mr. Dalton, Jan and Mary, Peggy, Britten, Jan again, Bessie before her actual murder, a reporter, a black couple he overhears, the men searching for him, and all the people at the inquest and at the trial. At several points, in fact, he includes himself as a victim in these fantasies: "He knew that the moment he allowed what his life meant to enter fully into his consciousness, he would seize some heavy object . . . and with one final blow blot it [Mary's car] out—with himself and them in it"; "He would shoot when they were closer and he would save one bullet for himself"; "There sprang up in him again the will to kill. But this time it was not directed outward toward people, but inward upon himself."

That is a lot of killing—but its function is not necessarily expressive. If one examines these killings, both real and imagined, in context one finds that each of them is in fact an instinctive response to fear, a means of escape from a physical or psychological threat, a survival strategy in the most direct sense. It is true that Bigger attempts to turn the killing of Mary to account after the fact, to attach expressive significance to the act in his memory. The act itself, however, is motivated by no such intention. In the page or so of text that recounts the first murder, Bigger and his feelings are described in the following terms: "hysterical terror," "fists clenched in fear," "afraid" (used twice), "fear," "frenzy," "frantically," and "intimidated to the core." These or similar terms accompany each of the accounts of Bigger's killings, real or imagined. Killing, in other words, is not a consciously chosen form of self-expression for Bigger but rather an involuntary consequence of his failure to express his feelings, his failure to understand and communicate his own fear, and thereby to disrupt "the rhythms of . . . indifference and violence" that rule his life.

The question still remains whether Bigger discovers any mode of expression capable of reunifying his dissociated sensibility and rendering him a whole human being. The answer is that the book itself, as a self-reflexive work of art, accomplishes that function. This success is a highly qualified one, however, for it is achieved only in the shadowy realm of virtual reality, of projected desire, and not in the realm actually inhabited by Bigger. As a human being, Bigger fails utterly to resolve the conflicting terms of his existence. What resolutions he achieves, he finds only by turning himself into a character and his life into art. This is not to imply that Bigger is somehow the author of the book—he emphatically is not. It is to say, rather, that the book is written in a manner consistent with an imaginative reality which Bigger struggles to create.

Irving Howe offers a useful observation in this regard in a 1963 essay which is often cited by critics, though generally for different reasons. Howe calls into question the conventional wisdom that classifies *Native Son* as a naturalistic novel in the tradition of Dreiser:

> *Native Son* is a work of assault rather than withdrawal; the author yields himself in part to a vision of nightmare. Bigger's cowering perception of the world becomes the most vivid and authentic component of the book. Naturalism pushed to an extreme turns here into something other than itself, a kind of expressionist outburst, no longer a replica of the familiar social world but a self-contained realm of grotesque emblems.

Howe never follows up the logic of this insight (ignores it, in fact, in the next paragraph which criticizes Wright's technique), but it is a logic which accommodates perfectly the central thematic concerns and which accounts at last for the book's excesses of characterization, plot, and narrative technique. It is, in effect, an expressionistic mode of composition which Wright describes in "How 'Bigger' Was Born" when he says,

> I restricted the novel to what Bigger saw and felt, to the limits of his feelings and thoughts, even when I was conveying *more* than that to the reader. I had the notion that such a manner of rendering made for a sharper effect, a more pointed sense of the character, his peculiar type of being and consciousness. Throughout there is but one point of view: Bigger's.

Wright's practice is consistent with this stated intention: he gives the reader not the world Bigger lives in but the world Bigger lives. He presents the world as Bigger feels and experiences it. The writer's task here is not simply a problem in the logistics of point of view (describing what Bigger actually sees or what it means to him given what he already knows), nor is it an exercise in creative hallucinations. Somewhere between the two lies a real and larger world, one seen through the distorting optic of fear. Bigger, again, is not the author of this book and there is much in it that he does not understand and could not have imagined independently, but its exaggerations, simplifications, and lack of proportion conform exactly to Bigger's "peculiar type of being and consciousness." It is the projection of this being and consciousness onto the world, and not what "really happens," that finally matters to Wright, to the readers, and especially to Bigger himself.

This technique of projection is most readily apparent in the depiction of characters. Wright acknowledges that he "gave no more reality to the other characters than that which Bigger himself saw," and Bigger sees only what his fear allows him to see. Bigger's interactions with others are conditioned by his efforts to meet expectations by conforming to type. He can do this only by first typing those for whom he must play his various roles. His visits to the movies may be seen in this light as research, and his playacting on the street with Gus as practice, in the serious business of human typology. The characters of the novel, apart from Bigger, are stereotypes because they are stereotypes for Bigger. They are individuals who have been reduced to what Bigger fears, needs, desires, and struggles to understand, and a different part of Bigger swings into action to meet the threat or, less often, the opportunity that each offers. Thus he is boastful with Buddy, tough with Gus, tender with Bessie, subservient with the Daltons, guarded with Jan, self-effacing with Britten, and so on. The reader sees what Bigger sees, a world full of typed characters even though some of them are types that Bigger has never met or identified before.

But all of this typing, both of self and of others, takes its toll. Bigger longs for genuine acceptance and understanding, though he continually frustrates this longing by the barriers he erects. His need to be something different to each is in tension with his need to be himself to all. This second and deeper need, long suppressed, eventually takes precedence, and the turning point depends upon a most improbable manipulation by the author: the scene in which a dozen characters all crowd into Bigger's jail cell. Wright himself comments on the implausibility of this scene in his introductory essay:

> While writing that scene, I knew it was unlikely that so many people would ever be allowed to come into a murderer's cell. But I wanted those people in that cell to elicit a certain important emotional response from Bigger. And so the scene stood.

What happens in that cell is that all of the distorted versions of Bigger represented by all of the characters in his life come together at once, and in the process a psychic critical mass is reached and exceeded. He must be several different Biggers at once, and he cannot do it:

> Desperately he cast about for something to say. Hate and shame boiled in him against the people behind his back; he

> tried to think of words that would defy them. . . . And at
> the same time he wanted those words to stop the tears of
> his mother and sister, to quiet and soothe the anger of his
> brother.

His solution is to assure his mother "I'll be out of this in no time," a statement which only shocks and embarrasses those whom it is intended to impress. Bigger is then forced to listen helplessly to a humiliating exchange among the characters in his life, the different parts of himself, that leaves him "weak and exhausted." He has seen that when all the separately maintained pieces of himself are brought together they make no sense and instead threaten to destroy him as an individual. After this scene, his conscious energy no longer focuses on maintaining his many outward guises but rather on the search for his own inner reality. His family returns once and he again lies to them, but he immediately rejects the lie, and the whole incident is reported briefly and indirectly. Otherwise, the little life that remains to him is devoted to his efforts to express a more authentic self-understanding.

The element of plot has the same function in the book as that of character, to project images that express Bigger's emotional experience. Plot, in part, supports character in this respect, for not only does it bring all the important surviving characters together in the crowded-cell scene, but it brings Bigger into contact in the first place, against all likelihood, with precisely those forces that he most fears and that most challenge his self-understanding, forces represented by the Daltons, Mary, Jan, Buckley, and Reverend Hammond. More importantly, it parallels the element of character in creating and arranging events which pose fundamental threats to Bigger at the same time that they serve his need to see his life as he really feels it. Like the characters, the events in the novel are "typed" events. They consist not of complex concatenations of forces and circumstances but of experience reduced to single emotions projected onto reality and objectified, haunting fantasies become real. The murder of Mary thereby becomes a concentrated, particular experience of fear, the disposal of her body one of dehumanization, the capture of Bigger on the water tower one of utter isolation and victimization, and so on. Bigger feels excluded from the conventional "picture of Creation" which, in his emotional core, he has "killed" and in its place "created a new world for himself." This "new world" is reflected in the book and its extravagant plot.

Not only do the events of the novel provide concrete images of Bigger's emotional experience, but they also work together to place him in a situation in which he is forced to contemplate them. As other critics have pointed out, in the "Fate" section Bigger has no choice but to shift from his customary active mode to an unwonted reflective one. And lest he turn away from his memory of these images, they are concretely reinforced, with all the emotional reality they embody, by new events, presented with the same expressionistic excess. He is, for example, taken from his cell to the Dalton home and told to reenact his crime. Though he refuses to put on a show (which seems to be the only intention of his jailers), he does indeed reenact, in his mind, his experience of "*that* night," and on leaving is shown a burning cross, spat upon, and made to listen to a crowd howling for his death. And in court, despite Bigger's plea of guilty, he must sit and listen as some sixty witnesses recount his crime in detail and watch as Mary's charred bones are displayed, the furnace from the Dalton home is reassembled, and the disposal of the body acted out for the jury.

All of these self-images are, of course, painful to Bigger, and he shrinks from them and yet is irresistibly drawn to them as well, for he recognizes them as the products of his own emotional experience. This becomes clear in part through the often heavy-handed foreshadowing found in the first section. It has often been observed that the killing of the rat prepares both Bigger and the reader for later killings, but the foreshadowing hardly stops there. Shortly after, in Bigger's hearing, Vera asks her mother the question that lies at the heart of the entire novel: "How come Bigger acts that way?" Her answer: "He's just . . . plain dumb black crazy." Later, on the street, Bigger tells Gus that being black in a white world is "just like living in jail" and admits "sometimes I feel like something awful's going to happen to me," a feeling which he then reformulates: "It's like I was going to do something I can't help." In the movie theater, he tells Gus "Say, maybe I'll be working for folks like that if I take that relief job. Maybe I'll be driving 'em around." He then goes on to predict almost exactly the situation in which he will find himself that evening:

Maybe Mr. Dalton was a millionaire. Maybe he had a daughter who was a hot kind of girl; maybe she spent lots of money; maybe she'd like to come to the South Side and see the sights sometimes. Or maybe she had a secret sweetheart and only he would know about it because he would have to drive her around; maybe she would give him money not to tell.

Bigger has thus already imagined the general direction as well as many of the specific details of the plot that is to unfold. Once the murder is accomplished, he confirms his feeling that he "had been dreaming of something like this for a long time, and then, suddenly, it was true," and reconfirms it as he begins his flight from justice: "All his life he had been knowing that sooner or later something like this would come to him. And now, here it was."

Bigger recognizes these events as expressive of his own emotional reality and contemplates them in fascination, and he will not be denied the opportunity for self-understanding that they represent. Repeatedly it occurs to Bigger that he had best escape, leave town, or at least shake down the ashes in the furnace in order to prevent Mary's remains from being discovered, and repeatedly he fails to do what he must to save himself from being caught. A blizzard at last conveniently seals off all exits from Chicago, and with them seals Bigger's fate. These "failures," however, are not the result of obtuseness on Bigger's part but of a compulsion to be a part of this plot until it plays itself out: "He was following a strange path into a strange land and his nerves were hungry to see where it led." In the Dalton house, before the discovery of Mary's body, "the thought that he had the chance to walk out of here and be clear of it all came to him, and again he brushed it aside. He was tensely eager to stay and see how it would all end, even if that end swallowed him in blackness." When Buckley suggests the possibility of an insanity plea to Bigger as a "way out," Bigger immediately responds, "I don't want no way out." Bigger seems, in fact, to be accepting and even hastening his own death. This impression is supported by Bigger's thoughts and fantasies of self-destruction as well as by other passages contributing to the same pattern: "He wished that they would shoot him so that he could be free of them forever"; "An organic wish to cease to be, to stop living, seized him"; Bigger's dream of his own severed head. The significance that this pattern takes on in the context of Bigger's urge to self-expression is not simply that of a "death wish." Rather it is a recognition that the conditions of his life exclude the very thing that his being requires: the freedom to express his individual human needs without fear. The consequence of an attempt to reweld his dissociated sensibility, despite this fundamental antithesis, is a kind of self-immolation. Bigger himself acknowledges the inevitability of this consequence: "It seems sort of natural-like, me being here facing that death chair. Now I come to think of it, it seems like something like this just had to be."

Like the characterization and plot, the narrative voice in *Native Son* serves as more than simply a technical support to a work of fiction. It too functions more particularly as an expressionistic projection of Bigger's sensibility. It not only expresses Bigger's dilemma, but in its particular mode of expression it concretely embodies that dilemma as well.

Broadly speaking, Bigger suffers from an inability to communicate a conscious understanding of his own emotional reality. In a narrower sense, Bigger lacks words and feels this lack as a potent form of alienation from others. James Nagel, commenting on "images of 'vision' in *Native Son*," suggests a similar insight, that only at the end does Bigger realize "that his real tragedy is not death; it is rather the fact of never having been clearly seen by anyone." This is spelled out most clearly when Bigger attempts to express himself to Max, the one person who has come closest to understanding him:

> He could not talk. . . . Max was upon another planet, far off in space. Was there any way to break down this wall of isolation? Distractedly he gazed about the cell, trying to remember where he had heard words that would help him. He could recall none. He had lived outside of the lives of men. Their modes of communication, their symbols and images, had been denied him.

The long-felt need to explain himself becomes at last, in the terms of the plot, a matter of physical survival, for he can finally do nothing to save himself but plead his case to the court, and yet "he knew that the moment he tried to put his feelings into words, his tongue would not move." This premonition proves true when Bigger is given the opportunity to speak in court before being sentenced: "He tried to open his mouth to answer, but could not. Even if he had the power of speech, he did not know what he could have said."

If Bigger cannot speak for himself, however, others can and do speak for him and in the process take from him a large measure of control over his own destiny and over the satisfaction of his own needs. One notices this disparity, for example, when Bigger applies for a job and Mr. and Mrs. Dalton discuss his case in his presence but outside his comprehension: "The long strange words they used made no sense to him; it was another language." The press, often an important pressure impelling the plot forward, is another repository of the power of words, one which Bigger imagines that he has tapped by the power of his own actions:

> The papers ought to be full of him now. It did not seem strange that they should be, for all his life he had felt that things had been happening to him that should have gone into them. But only after he had acted upon feelings which he had had for years would the papers carry the story, *his* story.

The power of the preacher to manipulate, through words, the images that hold meaning for Bigger's life has already been seen. But the most significant figure in this respect, of course, is the lawyer, Max, who promises Bigger, "I'll tell the judge all I can of how you feel and why," and who stands up in court before the assembled representatives of the world Bigger fears but needs, and announces, "*I* shall witness for Bigger Thomas." Max has been characterized by various readers as a mouthpiece for the Communist Party. In fact, he is much more importantly a mouthpiece for Bigger, a fantasy come true: he possesses a vast audience, commands the language (words, imagery, frame of reference) of that audience, and stands in a privileged forum from which to address it. In every sense of the word, he *represents* Bigger to the world in a way that Bigger could never represent himself.

What Max is to Bigger's fictional life, the narrator is to the artistic image that is projected out of that life. The narrator's facility with words and propensity for extended abstract analysis and complex syntax compensate—indeed, *over*compensate—for Bigger's stance of mute incomprehension before his own experience. As the novel proceeds, Bigger acts and feels while the narrator reasons aloud about these actions and feelings. The relationship is precisely the one described (by the narrator) between the two parts of Bigger as he lies in his cell awaiting trial: "Blind impulses welled up in his body, and his intelligence sought to make them plain to his understanding by supplying images that would explain them." The narrator speaks for Bigger just as Max does, supplying images to his impulses, mind to his body. Max's action is limited, however, and he does not succeed in his effort to explain Bigger. Because he lives in the same external world as Bigger, he faces the same barriers and threats. The "crazy" student in Bigger's cell is another example of someone who tries to express directly his understanding of reality and who suffers as a result. Bigger's only recourse, again, is to imagination, to art. Wright describes, in "How 'Bigger' Was Born," his intention to explain "everything only in terms of Bigger's life and, if possible, in the rhythms of Bigger's thought (even though the words would be mine)," acknowledging readily the range of technical and linguistic devices which contribute to this "explanation," a range which is utterly beyond Bigger's capabilities. And the narrator himself on occasion recognizes the differences between Bigger's voice and his own: "though he could not have put it into words, he felt that." Because Bigger cannot "reach out with his bare hands and carve from naked space the concrete solid reasons" for his actions, the narrator is created to carve those reasons from language, an equally resistant material for Bigger. There is nothing subtle about the narrator of *Native Son*: his comments are obtrusive, overwrought, and tendentious. He lacks sophistication. He is a literary cliché. And he is precisely the narrator Bigger would create, if he were able, to tell his story for him.

An enormous imaginative structure of characters, events, and narrative devices has been elaborated not merely to describe but to *express*, in the full sense of that word, the emotional experience of Bigger Thomas. The question which remains is whether this structure has been adequate either to repair or to circumvent Bigger's dissociated sensibility. There is a certain sense of failure implicit in any recourse to an expressionistic mode of writing, a despair at one's inability to make sense of experience that is fundamentally hostile to certain human needs or values. In *Native Son*, there seems to be a recognition of that failure or inadequacy built into the very terms of the work itself. In the first two sections, Bigger's persona expands to fill the world as he perceives it, and an extravagant sequence of characters, events, and commentaries provides him with images of his own experience. In the last section that sequence slows and eventually shuts itself off, leaving Bigger immobilized and forced—or free—to contemplate those images. Such contemplation is, in Bigger's terms, the function of the entire procedure. The original movement of expansion does not merely halt, however, but reverses itself as Bigger's persona collapses in on itself. As the trial plays itself out, Bigger's active experience becomes increasingly restricted and the *images* of his past experience take up exclusive and fixed residence inside his consciousness. His last hope for contact with others is cut off as Max backs away in terror from Bigger's dawning sense of "rightness." Gone too is any hope of escaping execution. All that is left in Bigger is a solipsistic acceptance of his own feelings, now beyond explanation or justification:

> What I killed for must've been good. . . . I can say it now, 'cause I'm going to die. I know what I'm saying real good and I know how it sounds. But I'm all right. I feel all right when I look at it that way.

Not only does Bigger have "the last word" over Max, as Irving Howe has so often been quoted to say, but over the narrator as well, who drops away at last because Bigger "can say it now" and knows what he is saying "real good." This final pathetic utterance, so triumphant in Bigger's mind, isolates him forever and leaves him clinging with a kind of desperate joy to the fear and hate that have destroyed his life.

Alienation and Creativity
in *Native Son*

Valerie Smith

The criticism of Wright's work commonly notes that his prose writings center on the figure of the outsider; the novelist focuses on protagonists who either cannot or will not conform to the expectations that figures of authority, whether black or white, impose on them. What concerns me about Wright is not so much that his protagonists are all rebel-victims or outsiders. Rather, I am interested in the strategies his characters use to come to terms with their isolation and their sense of the discontinuity of their lives. My analysis of *Native Son* demonstrates that for Bigger Thomas, the protagonist, as for the autobiographical Richard, learning to tell his own story gives him a measure of control over his life and releases him from his feelings of isolation. Bigger is an uneducated criminal, a far cry from young Richard Wright—the brilliant, sensitive, rather self-righteous budding artist. But both young men are able to heal the discontinuities of their lives by learning to use language to describe themselves.

From the beginning of the novel Bigger's alienation from his oppressive environment is evident. His family and friends—poor, frustrated, brutalized—are tantalized by the promise of the American Dream, a narrative of limitless possibilities that will never be theirs. To mitigate their frustration, Bigger's family and friends all participate in some kind of communal activity. His mother finds consolation

From *Self-Discovery and Authority in Afro-American Narrative*. © 1987 by the President and Fellows of Harvard College. Harvard University Press, 1987.

in religion, his friends and his girlfriend, Bessie, in drinking. Neither of these particular techniques of evasion satisfies Bigger, although he too seeks a way of alleviating his sense of marginality. As the narrator remarks, "He knew that the moment he allowed himself to feel to its fullness how they lived, the shame and misery of their lives, he would be swept out of himself with fear and despair."

On occasion Bigger avoids his "fear and despair" by blocking out another person's presence. When his family reminds him of their suffering, for example, "he shut their voices out of his mind." When tempted to consider ways of escaping his situation, he "stopped thinking" in order to avoid disappointment. And when at first the Daltons, his white employers, make him feel uncomfortable, Bigger wishes earnestly to "blot" out both himself and "the other[s]."

As his confrontation with his friend Gus shows, Bigger also tries to avoid his own suffering by displacing his self-hatred onto other people. Gus and Bigger argue violently over whether to rob a white-owned store. Bigger fears the consequences both of perpetrating a crime against a white person and of admitting that timidity to his friends. Unable to express his own trepidation, he assaults Gus when he appears reluctant. Bigger recognizes his own fear in Gus's hesitation, and attacks Gus in an effort to destroy it.

Bigger participates in various activities with his friends that insulate him from his fears and insecurities. They rob other black people because they know that to do so will not bring punishment. Moreover, they imagine themselves the protagonists of alternate plots that coincide with the American myth in a way that their own lives do not. When they "play white," for instance, they pretend to be millionaires or public officials, and momentarily forget their own powerlessness. Likewise, they live vicariously through the movies they see. Yet despite this ostensible camaraderie and the lure of fantasy, Bigger is alienated from his friends, for he fears acknowledging his feelings either to himself or to other people. In the words of the narrator: "As long as he could remember [Bigger] had never been responsible to anyone. *The moment a situation became so that it exacted something of him, he rebelled.* That was the way he lived; he passed his days trying to defeat or gratify powerful impulses in a world he feared" (emphasis mine).

In order to emphasize Bigger's passivity and fear of articulation in the early sections of the novel, Wright relies on an omniscient narrative presence to tell his reader what Bigger thinks. Since Bigger does not allow himself to think, to act, or to speak directly and openly, the narrator tells us the things Bigger cannot admit to himself, such as his reason for attacking Gus.

Bigger's fear of articulation is also shown in his response to the way strangers talk to him. Bigger is terrified by the Daltons when he arrives at their home. On the surface he seems to be intimidated by their wealth and power. But in fact his disorientation results from his inability to understand their language. When Mrs. Dalton suggests how the family should treat him, she uses a vocabulary that Bigger finds unintelligible and that ironically undercuts the very point she is trying to make: " 'I think it's important emotionally that he feels free to trust his environment,' the woman said. 'Using the analysis contained in the case record the relief sent us, I think we should evoke an immediate feeling of confidence.' " Unaccustomed to this kind of speech, Bigger finds her vocabulary threatening: "It made him uneasy, tense, as though there were influences and presences about him which he could feel but not see."

In several ways Bigger's killing of Mary Dalton transforms his personality. The murder, which Bigger has not planned, is ostensibly inadvertent; nevertheless, on a more profound level it is fully intended. Bigger has wanted to "blot" Mary out whenever she has made him feel self-conscious and disoriented. Her murder is therefore important to Bigger because it enables him to complete an action he has willed:

> *He* had done this. *He* had brought all this about. In all of his life this murder was the most meaningful thing that had ever happened to him. He was living, truly and deeply, no matter what others might think, looking at him with their blind eyes. Never had he had the chance to live out the consequences of his actions; never had his will been so free as in this night and day of fear and murder and flight.

The murder is also profoundly significant because it forces Bigger to confront the fear of the unknown, which has plagued him throughout his life. He and his friends never rob Blum, the white storekeeper, because for them, to commit a crime against a white person is to enter a realm of terror, an area variously referred to by the narrator as "territory where the full wrath of an alien white world would be turned loose upon them," a "shadowy region, a No Man's Land, the ground that separated the white world from the black." It is this

unexplored danger zone that Bigger fears and that he persists in
avoiding until he kills Mary Dalton. Once he has committed this
action, he advances into this gray area, this "No Man's Land"; he
realizes that at least initially this trespass has not destroyed him.
Indeed, the knowledge that he continues to exist even after he has
looked at the heart of darkness empowers him to achieve levels of
action and articulation that he had formerly been unable to attain.
Having been forced to look directly at that which had frightened him
the most, Bigger now begins to liberate himself from the fear that
haunts him. Although the murder makes him first a fugitive from and
then a prisoner of justice, it initiates the process by which he
ultimately comes to understand the meaning of his life.

Because the murder makes Bigger less fearful of the truth, it
enables him to understand his environment more clearly. He becomes
more analytical, and instead of blotting out his perceptions, he begins
to make fine discriminations. Over breakfast on the morning after the
murder, for example, he looks at his family as if with new eyes. He
sees in his brother's blindness "a certain stillness, an isolation,
meaninglessness." He perceives the nuances of his mother's de-
meanor: "Whenever she wanted to look at anything, even though it
was near her, she turned her entire head and body to see it and did not
shift her eyes. There was in her heart, it seemed, a heavy and
delicately balanced burden whose weight she did not want to assume
by disturbing it one whit." And he sees his sister's fear as if for the
first time: she "seemed to be shrinking from life in every gesture she
made. The very manner in which she sat showed a fear so deep as to
be an organic part of her; she carried the food to her mouth in tiny
bits, as if dreading its choking her, or fearing that it would give out
too quickly."

Moreover, Bigger begins to look at his own life more contem-
platively. He interprets what and how his life means by trying to
assign value to his past actions. He concludes that the murder was a
creative gesture because it has enabled him to refashion his life: "This
crime was an anchor weighing him safely in time." In addition, he
consciously decides to accept responsibility for an action that might be
considered accidental:

> Though he had killed by accident, not once did he feel the
> need to tell himself that it had been an accident. He was
> black and he had been alone in a room where a white girl

had been killed; therefore he had killed her. . . . It was no longer a matter of dumb wonder as to what would happen to him and his black skin; he knew now. The hidden meaning of his life—a meaning which others did not see and which he had always tried to hide—had spilled out.

Bigger's immediate response to the murder demonstrates the extent to which it has liberated him and sharpened his vision. Before the murder Bigger's imagination was inhibited by his fears; he generally preferred not to think. Immediately afterward, however, instead of blocking out the fact of the murder, he confronts and verbalizes it. He has a momentary impulse to run away, but he denies it. Instead of lapsing into his characteristically evasive behavior, he begins to plan his defense with a previously unrevealed freedom of mind. It would have been simple for Bigger to follow his first instincts and choose the more passive way out. Earlier in the evening he had been directed to take Mary's trunk to the basement before going home for the night. He could have proceeded as if nothing had gone wrong. He could have taken the trunk to the basement, put the car in the garage, and gone home. Instead, he decides to destroy the body and implicate Mary's boyfriend, Jan. Rather than choosing the path of least resistance, Bigger creates an elaborate story in order to save himself.

By identifying Jan (indirectly) as the kidnapper and burning Mary's body, Bigger actually seeks to return to and change the past. In a sense, it is as if Bigger takes the pen from Wright and rewrites his story into the tale he wants it to be. Bigger removes himself from the role of the protagonist and changes the nature of the crime to a kidnapping. He tries to create a substitute reality—that is, a fiction—to replace the one that threatens to destroy him. The extent of Bigger's investment in the story he creates is demonstrated in the way he embellishes it. He keeps searching for a better story, not merely the tightest excuse he can find: "Suppose he told them that he had come to get the trunk?—That was it! The *trunk!* His fingerprints had a right to be there. . . . He could take the trunk to the basement and put the car into the garage and then go home. *No!* There was a better way. He would say that Jan had come to the house and he had left Jan outside in the car. But there was still *a better way!* Make them think that Jan did it." The larger significance of Bigger's fiction making and its similarity to young Richard's impulse to write reveals itself if we consider that he has suffered throughout his life from other people's attempts to impose their fictions—stereotypes—on him. Precisely because whites insist on seeing Bigger as less than human, he cannot enjoy the privileges that should be his. Dalton, who is sufficiently myopic to believe that he can be at once a slumlord and a philanthropist, fails to recognize Bigger (or any black person) as fully human. Instead, to him black people are objects of charity easily placated with ping-pong tables. His wife responds to Bigger as if he were a sociological case study. And although Mary and Jan pride themselves on their radical politics, they never really see Bigger either. They treat him as if he and his people were curiosities. They sing spirituals and use black colloquialisms in order to exhibit their familiarity with what are to them exotic artifacts. They insist on eating with Bigger at a black-owned restaurant, oblivious to the discomfort that may cause him. That Jan and Mary use Bigger as a means of access to certain experiences, with no awareness of his feelings, shows that they too see Bigger as their own creation, not as what Bigger himself actually is.

Bigger's misrepresentation in court and in the press epitomizes his lifelong struggle against other people's fictions. Buckley, the State's Attorney, considers him to be violent and subhuman and prosecutes him according to collectively held stereotypes of black male behavior. To him the specific details of Bigger's case are uninteresting, irrelevant. Bigger is guilty of one count of second-degree murder (Mary's) and one count of first-degree murder (Bessie's). The State's Attorney, however, considers Bessie's murder significant only insofar as it provides evidence that he can use to reconstruct Mary's death. He successfully prosecutes Bigger for raping Mary on the assumption that black men are driven to possess white women sexually. Moreover, he assumes that Bigger killed Mary to hide the fact that he had raped her. The press similarly denies Bigger's individuality, referring to him with such epithets as "jungle beast" and "missing link." Indeed, the journalists insist that Bigger, a black man, could not be smart enough to have committed his crimes without the assistance of white co-conspirators. They argue that Communists helped him plot his crime, because "the plan of the murder and kidnapping was too elaborate to be the work of a Negro mind."

Bigger's complex defense signals his ability to articulate a story about himself that challenges the one that others impose on him. But his story has its limitations and does not accomplish all that Bigger intends. At this stage in his life, he, like the young Richard Wright, recognizes that language has power, but he does not yet know how to use it.

In his naiveté Bigger patterns his tale on pulp detective fiction. The story, based on poorly written models, depends on too many narrative inconsistencies. Bigger does not, for example, remember that Jan left him and Mary in order to go to a party and will therefore have an alibi. What is perhaps more important, however, is that Bigger's first story (like the ex-colored man's narrative) fails him because he uses it as a technique of evasion. Although his experience has helped him face his situation, he uses his story to help him escape it.

As I have pointed out, during the period when Bigger is most timid and self-protective (before he arrives at the Dalton home), his consciousness is most restrained, and Wright relies on an omniscient narrator to explain his character's thoughts and motivations. As Bigger's imagination and emotions spring to life, ironically after he kills Mary, Wright relies increasingly on free indirect discourse. In other words, as Bigger's capacity to understand and express himself increases, Wright allows him to speak for himself. Even though Bigger is terrified by the thought of seeing Mary's bones, for example, he can at least acknowledge his fear; he has moved beyond the point of denying his trepidation. As a result, Wright presents his consciousness by approximating Bigger's thoughts:

> He stood a moment looking through the cracks into the humming fire, blindingly red now. But how long would it keep that way, if he did not shake the ashes down? He remembered the last time he had tried and how hysterical he had felt. He must do better than this. . . . For the life of him, he could not bring himself to shake those ashes. But did it really matter? No. . . . No one would look into the bin. Why should they?

Similarly, Bigger comprehends the significance of his inability to retrieve his money from Bessie's dress pocket after he has thrown her down the air shaft: "*Good God!* Goddamn, yes, it was in her dress pocket! Now, he was in for it. He had thrown Bessie down the air-shaft and the money was in the pocket of her dress! What could he do about it? Should he go down and get it? Anguish gripped him. . . . He did not want to see her again. . . . Well, he would have to do without money; that was all."

As long as Bigger is a fugitive from the law, he thinks quickly and improvises plans to remain free. When his capture is imminent and Bigger realizes that his future will be even more closely confined than his past, his earlier fears descend on him again and he resumes his former passive, evasive behavior. When his pursuers corner him, Bigger gives up his sense of wholeness and returns to his earlier unresponsiveness. Gradually he steps outside of himself, watching his capture as if from behind a curtain and then ignoring it as if he is standing behind a wall. As his captors drag him downstairs, he completes this dissociation by forcing himself to lose consciousness.

Bigger tries but fails to pass his final days in this unresponsive condition. At first he refuses to eat, to drink, to smoke, to resist, and "steadfastly [refuses] to speak." He tries to avoid thinking and feeling as well, because he assumes that his one leap of faith has caused his defeat: "Why not kill that wayward yearning within him that had led him to this end? He had reached out and killed and had not solved anything, so why not reach inward and kill that which had duped him?" When he is bombarded with faces and with the reality of his situation, Bigger faints at his inquest. But when he regains consciousness a second time, his recently acquired sense of himself (the narrator calls it "pride,") returns, and Bigger begins to rebuild that bridge of words that once connected him with other people. He insists on reading a newspaper because he cannot understand his position until he knows what others are saying about him. More important than his reading, however, are the conversations Bigger has with Jan, Buckley, and Max, the attorney from the Labor Defenders who is in charge of Bigger's defense. Each interview or exchange teaches him something about communication and about himself.

In his conversation with Jan, Bigger conquers his fear of self-scrutiny. Indeed, in his subsequent conversations he attempts to use language to make himself understood with the same clarity he achieves with Jan. By admitting that he and Mary had humiliated Bigger inadvertently, and by offering to help him, Jan enables Bigger to overcome his defenses. His words take Bigger outside of himself and allow him to feel his humanity.

This conversation restores and heightens Bigger's faith in the power of language. Because of this exchange, Bigger does not retreat from his family when they visit him. Instead, he searches for the right words both to comfort them and to defy the authorities. His first attempt to speak to them is unsatisfactory: he tries to dismiss cavalierly the extremity of his situation. But his conversation with Jan has impressed upon Bigger the necessity of candor; Bigger retracts these defensive comments, replacing them with words that express his resignation.

His confession to Buckley teaches Bigger an additional lesson about the necessity of articulation. Buckley's interrogation consists essentially of a series of true-or-false questions. He accuses Bigger of numerous crimes and tries to make him confess to them. Because Buckley seems so eager to pin offenses on him that he never committed, Bigger is forced to defend himself and tell his story as it happened. The effect of articulating this story to a hostile listener drains Bigger; he fears that he may have made himself excessively vulnerable by telling his enemy the truth. But as the narrator suggests, the ostensible ordeal of telling his story actually propels Bigger on to a higher level of self-knowledge:

> He lay on the cold floor sobbing; but really he was standing up strongly with contrite heart, holding his life in his hands, staring at it with a wondering question. He lay on the cold floor sobbing; but really he was pushing forward with his puny strength against a world too big and too strong for him. He lay on the cold floor sobbing; but really he was groping forward with fierce zeal into a welter of circumstances which he felt contained a water of mercy for the thirst of his heart and brain.

If Bigger's confession to Buckley is important because it enables him to tell what really happened, his confession to Max in a parallel scene is important because it enables him to tell why it happened. Talking to Max allows Bigger to understand for the first time the complex feelings he had for Mary. The search for the appropriate words is a painful and gradual one for him; remembering Mary triggers "a net of vague, associative" memories of his sister. And ultimately, he gives up "trying to explain" his actions logically and reverts "to his feelings as a guide in answering Max." But as he traces his thoughts and anxieties, Bigger becomes conscious for the first time of certain feelings, and he expresses to Max emotions that had been intensely private. For example, during his conversation he first understands the relationship between the frustration he has always felt and his violence toward Mary. Moreover, on this occasion he admits to someone else that he lost control of himself at the moment he killed Mary. Most important, he is able to explain the value of the murder: that it freed him from his lifelong fears. While Bigger felt helpless and betrayed after confessing to Buckley, explaining himself to Max gives him an enormous sense of relief. That "urge to talk" had been so strong within him that he had felt "he ought to be able to reach out with his bare hands and carve from naked space the concrete solid reasons why he had murdered." Telling his story helps him understand those reasons and grants him a "cold breath of peace" that he had never known before.

Wright's protagonists tend to fit a particular mold. Fishburn notes that the protagonists of Wright's later writings are all patterned after his autobiographical identity: "The young Richard Wright, like all his later heroes, must wrench his identity from a hostile environment; neither Wright nor his heroes have the comfort of being accepted by their own race. All are aliens among both the whites and the blacks." And in "Self-Portraits by Richard Wright," John M. Reilly comments that in *Black Boy* and "The Man Who Lived Underground," "a common viewpoint is that of the outsider in defensive flight from forces in the environment that threaten the personality."

Certainly Bigger suffers alienation from blacks and whites in the way that the autobiographical persona of *Black Boy* and *American Hunger* does. I would suggest a further parallel, however: like this other protagonist, Bigger comes to understand the power of language as a means of creating an identity for himself in an alien environment. Young Richard achieves the greater success; his talent for writing liberates him from the oppression of both the black and the white communities. But Bigger develops the capacity to use language as a way of confronting directly the truths of his own experience. Although it does not save him from electrocution, the capacity to explain himself to others provides him with an awareness of what his life has meant.

The Re(a)d and the Black

Barbara Johnson

> It is not surprising that this
> novel plumbs blacker depths of
> human experience than American
> literature has yet had.
>
> DOROTHY CANFIELD FISHER

In the fall of 1937, Richard Wright published an essay entitled "Blueprint for Negro Writing" in *New Challenge*, a little left-wing magazine he was helping to edit with Marian Minus and Dorothy West. In that essay he characterized previous Negro writing as "humble novels, poems, and plays, prim and decorous ambassadors who went a-begging to white America." He urged Negro writers to abandon the posture of humility and the bourgeois path of "individual achievement," and to develop a collective voice of social consciousness, both nationalist and Marxist. "The Negro writer must realize within the area of his own personal experience those impulses which, when prefigured in terms of broad social movements, constitute the stuff of nationalism. . . . It is through a Marxist conception of reality and society that the maximum degree of freedom in thought and feeling can be gained for the Negro writer." Negro writing, in other words, could fulfill itself only by becoming at once black and red.

Three years later, Wright published a novel that seemed to carry out this design, one that transformed the avuncular diminutions of previous Negro writing (including his own) into a larger and bolder form of assertion, changing the uncle, Tom, into a bigger Thomas. *Native Son* presents a new social archetype of American hunger, one that attempts to view the distorted strength of the black folk hero through the lens of a communist defense. Yet the merger between the red and the black is as problematic in the novel as it came to be for Richard Wright in life. What the Communist lawyer, Max, cannot hear is precisely Bigger's "I am," his ascension to the status of speaking subject:

> Bigger saw Max back away from him with compressed lips. But he felt he had to make Max understand how he saw things now.
>
> "I didn't want to kill!" Bigger shouted. "But what I killed for, I *am*! It must've been pretty deep in me to make me kill! I must have felt it awful hard to murder. . . ."
>
> Max lifted his hand to touch Bigger, but did not.
>
> "No; no; no. . . . Bigger, not that. . . ." Max pleaded despairingly.

What is it about Bigger that cannot be re(a)d within the perspective of Ma(r)x?

Max's understanding of Bigger's two murders places them squarely within the perspective of economic determinism. As Max tells the court, Bigger kills because other channels of self-expression are closed to him:

> Listen: what Bigger Thomas did early that Sunday morning in the Dalton home and what he did that Sunday night in that empty building was but a tiny aspect of what he had been doing all his life long! He was *living*, only as he knew how, and as we have forced him to live. The actions that resulted in the death of those two women were as instinctive and inevitable as breathing or blinking one's eyes. It was an act of *creation!*

It has often been assumed that Bigger's crimes can therefore be seen as that which, in the novel, stands in the place of *art*. Bigger is an artist with no medium to work in other than violence.

But is this actually the case? It will be my contention that there is in fact, within the novel itself, another sort of "Blueprint for Negro Writing," one that complicates the notion of a creativity "as instinctive and inevitable as breathing or blinking one's eyes" (indeed, one that makes even breathing and blinking the eyes into signifying acts that are not merely instinctual).

For Bigger, in fact, does not merely kill. He also writes. He writes a ransom note to the father of the white woman he has inadvertently killed. That note, and the scene of its writing, can be read in a way that exceeds its contextual function. And the reception of that text turns out to be as telling as its creation.

The scene of writing begins with the silencing of Bessie, the black woman whose involvement with Bigger will soon prove fatal to her.

> "I ain't asking you but once more to shut up!" he said,
> pushing the knife out of the way so he could write.

Substituting the pencil for the knife, Bigger performs an elaborate ritual of concealment, self-protection, and disguise:

> He put on the gloves and took up the pencil in a trembling hand and held it poised over the paper. He should disguise his handwriting. He changed the pencil from his right to his left hand. He would not write it; he would print it. He swallowed with dry throat.

Bigger's writing is designed to betray no trace of origin or signature. He is then faced with the question of pronoun: is his writing to be individual or collective? This is indeed the question Richard Wright has put before the Negro writer who wishes to write on the "left."

> Now, what would be the best kind of note? He thought, I want you to put ten thousand. . . . Naw; that would not do. Not "I." It would be better to say "we."

Instead of proceeding directly to his demand ("I want you to put ten thousand. . . ."), Bigger now makes up a story for the benefit of the addressee, the white male reader, leading with what he knows to be Mr. Dalton's concern:

> *We got your daughter*, he printed slowly in big round letters. That was better. He ought to say something to let Mr. Dalton think that Mary was still alive. He wrote: *She is safe.* Now, tell him not to go to the police. No! Say something about Mary first! He bent and wrote: *She wants to come home.* . . .

As he continues the note, he makes a crucial textual revision:

> Now, tell him not to go to the police. *Don't go to the police if you want your daughter back safe.* Naw; that ain't good. His scalp tingled with excitement; it seemed that he could feel each strand of hair upon his head. He read the line over and crossed out "safe" and wrote "alive."

What Bigger's visceral reaction demonstrates is his knowledge that his own fate is bound to the way in which his writing is linked, in the implied reader's mind, with the fate of a white woman. It is precisely Bigger's belief in the white father's inability to think his daughter safe that has led to her not being alive in the first place. Bigger implicitly feels the significance of his revision and all that needs to be revised behind it:

> For a moment he was frozen, still. There was in his stomach a slow, cold, vast rising movement, as though he held within the embrace of his bowels the swing of planets through space. He was giddy. He caught hold of himself, focused his attention to write again.

The details of the ransom drop follow. The only part of the note he pronounces "good" comes to him from another text:

> Now, about the money. How much? Yes; make it ten thousand. *Get ten thousand in 5 and 10 bills and put it in a shoe box.* . . . That's good. He had read that somewhere. . . . *and tomorrow night ride your car up and down Michigan Avenue from 35th Street to 40th Street.* That would make it hard for anybody to tell just where Bessie would be hiding. He wrote: *Blink your headlights some. When you see a light in a window blink three times throw the box in the snow and drive off. Do what this letter say.* Now, he would sign it. But how? It should be signed in some way that would throw them off the trail. Oh, yes! Sign it "Red." He printed, *Red.*

Like Richard Wright himself in 1940, Bigger is compelled to sign his writing "Red." Yet the note is signed "Black" as well: "*Do what this letter say.*" Hidden behind the letter's detour through communism is the unmistakable stylistic trace of its black authorship. Yet no one in the novel seems to be able to read it. In passing under the signature "Red," the text's blackness is precisely what goes unread. Bigger is in fact present at the scene of the letter's reception, but he remains unseen, "nobody."

The door swung in violently. Bigger started in fright. Mr.
Dalton came into the kitchen, his face ashy. He stared at
Peggy and Peggy, holding a dish towel in her hand, stared
at him. In Mr. Dalton's hand was the letter, opened.

"What's the matter, Mr. Dalton?"

"Who. . . . Where did. . . . Who gave you this?"

"What?"

"This *letter*."

"Why, nobody. I got it from the door."

"When?"

"A few minutes ago. Anything wrong?"

Mr. Dalton looked around the entire kitchen, not at
anything in particular, but just round the entire stretch of
four walls, his eyes wide and unseeing.

Like Poe's purloined letter, the identity of the author of the note
remains invisible because the detectives do not know how to read
what is plainly there before them. Behind the sentence "*Do what this
letter say*" lies the possibility—and the invisibility—of a whole vernacular literature.

If Bigger's ransom note represents in some sense black vernacular
literature, does this mean that in the writing of black men the life and
death of white womanhood is at stake? It is clear that this is the story
the white fathers will listen to. Indeed, whatever the facts, it seems
that this is the *only* story they will hear. This is what Bigger believes
as he stands over the bed of the intoxicated Mary, watching the blind
Mrs. Dalton approach. What *must not happen* is that he be caught alone
in the bedroom of a white woman. He forces a pillow over Mary's
face in order to prevent her from betraying his presence. Like
Oedipus, it is through his efforts to *avoid* enacting the forbidden story
that he inevitably enacts it. Like Oedipus, he participates in a primal
scene of, and with, blindness.

The name of the forbidden story in America is "rape." In an
essay entitled "How 'Bigger' Was Born," Wright describes his
growing awareness of the character type he wished to portray. As for
the plot, it was already scripted by American society:

Any Negro who has lived in the North or the South knows
that times without number he has heard of some Negro boy
being picked up on the streets and carted off to jail and
charged with "rape." This thing happens so often that to

my mind it had become a representative symbol of the
Negro's uncertain position in America. Never for a second
was I in doubt as to what kind of social reality or dramatic
situation I'd put Bigger in, what kind of test-tube life I'd
set up to evoke his deepest reactions. Life had made the plot
over and over again, to the extent that I knew it by heart.

("How 'Bigger' Was Born")

As many commentators have noted, the myth of the black rapist is an
inversion of historical fact: the fact that black slave women were so
commonly raped by their white owners. Yet Bigger Thomas does not
rape Mary Dalton; he kills her because he thinks that the only possible
interpretation of his presence in her room is "rape." It is not
surprising that the first edition of *Native Son* should have been
preceded by an introduction written by Dorothy Canfield Fisher. The
envelope of Wright's letter had to be made to say "The white woman
is safe."

To the extent that the rape of Mary Dalton does not occur, the
"rape" plot in *Native Son* may be read in terms of racist overdetermination. But what can be said about the fate of Bessie Mears, the
black woman who *is* raped by Bigger, and whose murder is far from
accidental? Is the rape and murder of a black woman somehow a
correlative to the black man's quest for manhood, a figure for the
defeminization Wright calls for in his blueprint for a literature that
would no longer go "curtsying to show that the Negro was not
inferior" ("Blueprint for Negro Writing")? If the novel makes a plea
for Bigger's victimization, does it implicitly excuse his treatment of
the black woman? Does racism explain away the novel's careless
misogyny?

It would be easy to attack Richard Wright for placing violence, as
James Baldwin puts it, in the space where sex should be. It would be
easy to read *Native Son*'s depiction of the relations between black men
and black women as unhealably troubled; indeed, to read the novel as
itself an act of violence against black women. I would like to shift the
ground of this interpretation slightly in order to ask: where, in
Richard Wright, does the black woman stand with respect to the black
man's *writing*?

As we have seen, Bessie Mears is a silent (silenced) presence in the
scene in which Bigger Thomas writes. As Bigger completes the
ransom note, he lifts his eyes and sees Bessie standing behind him.

She has read the note over his shoulder and guessed the truth. She looked straight into his eyes and whispered, "Bigger, did you kill that girl?" Bigger denies that she has interpreted his writing correctly, but he formulates a plan to kill her to prevent her from saying what she knows. The black woman, then, is a reader—a reader whose reading is both accurate and threatening.

Bigger's ransom note is not the only example in Richard Wright's work of a paradigmatic scene of writing in which what is at stake is the death of a nonblack woman. To this scene I would like to juxtapose a scene from Wright's autobiography, *Black Boy*. One of his earliest attempts at writing, he tells us, was the story of a beautiful Indian maiden.

> I remembered a series of volumes of Indian history I had read the year before. Yes, I knew what I would do; I would write a story about the Indians. . . . But what about them? Well, an Indian girl. . . . I wrote of an Indian maiden, beautiful and reserved, who sat alone upon the bank of a still stream, surrounded by eternal twilight and ancient trees, waiting. . . . The girl was keeping some vow which I could not describe and, not knowing how to develop the story, I resolved that the girl had to die. She rose slowly and walked toward the dark stream, her face stately and cold; she entered the water and walked on until the water reached her shoulders, her chin; then it covered her. Not a murmur or a gasp came from her, even in dying.

Writing in the illustrious tradition of Hawthorne, Poe, Wordsworth, Lamartine, and hundreds of other white men of letters, Wright has no difficulty seeing the death of an idealized woman as a significant literary subject. Not all male writers are candid enough, however, to admit that their heroine's untimely death is the result of a failure of imagination. "Not knowing how to develop the story, I resolved that the girl had to die." One wonders whether this might explain the early demise of Lucy or Annabel Lee—or even of Edna Pontellier.

But dead women are not the only women present in these scenes of writing, and in both cases the "other woman" is a black female reader whose reading cannot be mastered by the writer. As we have seen, Bessie reads Bigger's ransom note and begins to suspect that he has killed Mary Dalton. Later, his scheme thwarted, Bigger first rapes then kills Bessie in order to prevent her from talking, in order to gain total control over a story that has been out of his control from the beginning. In the case of the Indian maiden, Wright excitedly decides to read his literary creation to a young woman who lives next door.

> I interrupted her as she was washing dishes and, swearing her to secrecy, I read the composition aloud. When I finished she smiled at me oddly, her eyes baffled and astonished.
>
> "What's that for?" she asked.
>
> "Nothing," I said.
>
> "But why did you write it?"
>
> "I just wanted to."
>
> "Where did you get the idea?"
>
> I wagged my head, pulled down the corners of my mouth, stuffed my manuscript into my pocket and looked at her in a cocky manner that said: Oh, it's nothing at all. I write stuff like this all the time. It's easy, if you know how. But I merely said in an humble, quiet voice:
>
> "Oh, I don't know. I just thought it up."
>
> "What're you going to do with it?"
>
> "Nothing."
>
> God only knows what she thought. My environment contained nothing more alien than writing or the desire to express one's self in writing. But I never forgot the look of astonishment and bewilderment on the young woman's face when I had finished reading and glanced at her. Her inability to grasp what I had done or was trying to do somehow gratified me. Afterwards whenever I thought of her reaction I smiled happily for some unaccountable reason.

It would be hard to imagine a scene of reading in which less was understood. It is entirely possible that the woman was indeed wondering why Wright was writing at all. It is also possible that she was wondering why he was writing about the death of a woman. It is even possible that she was wondering why *he* wasn't wondering that.

What Wright's writing demonstrates again and again is the deadly effect both of overdetermination and of underdetermination in storytelling. It is because the "rape" plot is so overdetermined that Bigger becomes a murderer. It is because there are so few available models for the plots of Indian maidens that Wright's heroine "has to die." And it is because the "rape" plot about white women or the "idealization" plot about Indian women are so overdetermined that the plot about black women remains muffled beyond recognition. When the black woman does attempt to take control of her own plot in Wright's short story "Long Black Song," the black man dies in an apocalyptic fire. The unavailability of new plots is deadly. As Wright says of his Indian maiden composition, "I was excited; I read it over and saw that there was a yawning void in it. There was no plot, no action, nothing save atmosphere and longing and death."

Yet even when a black woman's story *is* available, there is no guarantee that it will be recognized. Upon reading Zora Neale Hurston's *Their Eyes Were Watching God*, Wright was able to see only red, not black; male, not female. "The sensory sweep of her novel," he wrote, "carries no theme, no message, no thought." The black woman's story can remain invisible no matter how visible it is, like the black vernacular origin of Bigger's ransom note. No reader has a monopoly on blindness. But Wright's blindness here is far from simple.

In a surprising and fascinating passage in Wright's essay "How 'Bigger' Was Born," we encounter the announcement of a novel that was never to reach completion: "I am launching out upon another novel, this time about the status of women in American society." The desire to tell a woman's story seems to infuse Wright's writing from the beginning. Yet however aborted the plots of his women protagonists, the figure of the black woman as *reader* in his work is fundamental. Silent, baffled, or filled with a dangerous insight, Wright consistently sees the black woman as the reader his writing must face. *Native Son*, indeed, is dedicated to Wright's own paralyzed mother.

Composing Bigger: Wright and the Making of *Native Son*

Joseph T. Skerrett, Jr.

More is going on in *Native Son* than a merely intellectual synthesis of literary naturalism and Marxist political economy. In an early review Malcolm Cowley sensed a widening of Wright's sympathies since the stories of *Uncle Tom's Children*, "a collection of stories all but one of which had the same pattern: a Negro was goaded into killing one or more white men and was killed in turn, without feeling regret for himself or his victims." Admiring the stories, Cowley thought them "painful to read," for he felt that in them Wright's indignation was expressing itself in the revenge of "a whole series of symbolic murders." "In *Native Son* the pattern is the same, but the author's sympathies have broadened and his resentment, though quite as deep, is less painful and personal." This suggestion that the intellectualization of the violent relationships portrayed in the short stories was doing something *for* Wright as well as for the reader is bolstered by Saunders Redding's insistence that Wright himself was behind Bigger Thomas's inarticulateness. Redding broadly asserted that "in a way that is more direct than is true of most important modern authors of fiction, Wright's heroes were in naked honesty himself, and not imaginary creations that served to express his complicated personality." Stanley Edgar Hyman accounted for the great power of *Native Son* by concluding that in the novel

> the tensions and guilts connected with sexuality, openly
> and deliberately manipulated in the fiction, fled into the

color imagery, and gave it a sexual resonance and ambiguity not consciously contrived, which powerfully reflected the social undercurrents of American life.

Despite these strong indications of alternative directions of inquiry, critics have been reluctant to release the by now comfortable grasp they have on the "protest fiction" aspect of Native Son. It has, I think, blinded them to the meaning of Native Son as the culmination of Wright's first phase as a writer. Native Son is not only Wright's most ambitious and most achieved work of art, but it is also the work in which he most completely—whether or not "openly and deliberately" as Hyman says—related the materials of his personal biography to his intellectual and aesthetic activities. In the working out of Native Son Wright objectified, in symbolic terms, the conflicts and passions arising out of his life up to that time. Native Son is rooted in the fertile soil of his personal psychosocial and psychosexual "situation," to use Kenneth Burke's term.

II

Wright began to work on the story before leaving Chicago for New York in the spring of 1939; one of his Chicago acquaintances at that time later told Michel Fabre that he could remember having seen a draft of early parts of the story shortly before Wright left for New York. In Chicago Wright had been living with his family—his ailing mother, his brother, and grandmother Wilson, who had joined them during the summer of 1934. If the emotional record of Black Boy is to be trusted, as I think it may, Wright must have felt the continual pressure of aggression and guilt and responsibility. Age had not tempered his grandmother's religious zeal and narrow-mindedness, and Wright's mother, though supportive, "was still partially paralyzed after a recent attack of encephalitis." Neither can have approved of whatever hint they got of Richard's involvement with the Communists. Wright respected his mother, Fabre says, "Because of her indisputable moral authority, [but] her devoutness irritated him more and more, along with her resigned attitude toward social injustice and hatred of communism." His dependent and seemingly indolent brother Leon did not contribute to the support of the family; "Wright spent increasingly less time at home in order to avoid friction between them." The intrafamiliar tensions so vividly described in *Black Boy* continued to exert pressure on Wright's life, even as, through his contact with the Communists, he was discovering a community which valued his rebellious attitudes. Wright's imaginative response to this complex "situation" was an equally complex one, for at the same time, at various stages of development, in 1934, 1935, and 1936 he was at work on the "objective" description of Jake Jackson's day in *Lawd Today*, the "ameliorative" and integrationist stories of *Uncle Tom's Children*; and the "revolutionary" attitudes of Bigger Thomas.

In "How 'Bigger' Was Born" Wright indicates that he sat down to his typewriter sometime in 1934 with the meaning and characterization of Bigger all "thought out." Whether this is true or not, the cathartic event in the process of committing Bigger to paper was Wright's new job at the South Side Youth Club. Here he was able to observe the rebellious urbanized and alienated black youths of whom Bigger is a composite and symbolic projection. But more importantly, at the Youth Club Wright began to identify with the passions of the delinquents and, as Fabre remarks, "for once, to give free reign to his own antisocial feelings." He felt that the job had thrust him into "a kind of dressed-up police work" and he hated the work of distracting these potential rebels with "ping-pong, checkers, swimming, marbles and baseball in order that [they] might not roam the streets and harm the valuable white property which adjoined the Black Belt." Privately Wright identified with the damage and disturbance the boys caused when they left his clubhouse in the afternoons, for it was a meaningful demonstration that "life is stronger than ping-pong." This identification with the criminal rebellion of his youthful charges enabled him to tolerate the work: "that was the only way I could contain myself for doing a job I hated; for a moment I'd allow myself, vicariously, to feel as Bigger felt—not much, just a little, just a *little*—but still, there it was" ("How 'Bigger' Was Born").

In giving rein to even this littlest amount of fellow-feeling with the boys and with his own imaginative re-creation of them, Wright brought himself face to face with his own inner tension about literary expression. He thought of literature as an essentially criminal activity, which had to be carried out under the shadow of what he calls in "How 'Bigger' Was Born" a "mental censor—product of the fears which a Negro feels from living in America." The fear of disapproval from white audiences and black leaders, though he considers them in separate categories, are really one and the same: fear of reprisal for the act of aggression he knew the book to be. The writing of the novel became entangled with Wright's deepest aggressive drives. His dissatisfaction with the response to *Uncle Tom's Children* supports this contention, for he found that it inspired more pity than terror.

> I found that I had written a book which even bankers' daughters could read and weep over and feel good about. I swore to myself that if I ever wrote another book, no one would weep over it; that it would be so hard and deep that they would have to face it without the consolation of tears.
>
> ("How 'Bigger' Was Born")

This feeling that the stories had failed was not a reflection of disapproval from Wright's Communist friends: their approval had been unstinting. The disapproval arose from within: the stories did not do for Wright what he wanted from them. So it was shortly after the completion of *Uncle Tom's Children* that Bigger Thomas, spawned in Wright's memories of "bad" black boys in his Mississippi home and developed in his observation of other boys in the Chicago slums, made contact with Wright's deepest personal fears and obsessions and took possession of his imagination: the writing of the novel became a struggle of exorcism from the forces, both black and white, that attempted to censor Wright's feeling of it.

> The more I thought of it the more I became convinced that if I did not write of Bigger as I saw and felt him, if I did not try to make him a living personality and at the same time a symbol of all the larger things I felt and saw in him, I'd be reacting as Bigger himself reacted: that is, I'd be acting out of *fear* if I let what I thought whites would say constrict and paralyze me.
>
> As I contemplated Bigger and what he meant, I said to myself: "I must write this novel, not only for others to read, but to free *myself* of his sense of shame and fear." In fact the novel, as time passed, grew upon me to the extent that it became a necessity to write it; the writing of it turned into a way of living for me.
>
> ("How 'Bigger' Was Born")

III

Bigger Thomas's situation in the novel is an imaginative replication of Wright's own "situation." Trapped by the economics of the Depression and the resultant intensification of racial prejudice and discrimination, Bigger feels resentment against the demands of his family—his religious mother, his sister Vera, and his younger brother, Buddy—whose needs require that he submit to the near-slavery of the employment offered by the welfare relief program. Bigger struggles against the family strategies to control his actions without access to the violence that is characteristic of his behavior later in the story. His central counter-strategy is to numb himself to the family feeling within:

> He shut their voices out of his mind. He hated his family because he knew that they were suffering and that he was powerless to help them. He knew that the moment he allowed himself to feel to its fullness how they lived, the shame and misery of their lives, he would be swept out of himself with fear and despair. So he held toward them an attitude of iron reserve; he lived with them, but behind a wall, a curtain.
>
> *(Native Son)*

This denial is, of course, not without its cost. Bigger must repress his own impulses even more stringently. "He knew that the moment he allowed what his life meant to enter fully into his consciousness, he would either kill himself or someone else. So he denied himself and acted tough."

Like Jake in *Lawd Today*, Bigger hesitates to follow out his occasional thoughts of rebellion. Each time he asks himself the question What can I do? "his mind hit[s] a blank wall and he [stops] thinking." Jake takes out his frustration and anger on his wife Lil, whom he blames for his troubles; Bigger is in many ways psychologically more sensitive. He has displaced his sensitivity and potential tenderness within the family circle in order to protect his ego from pain. Curiously, unlike Jake, Bigger has no symbolic outlet for his aggressive feeling, as Jake does in the elaborate verbal play of "the dozens" in which he engages his street buddy. Bigger's passion is too close to the surface, perhaps, to be assuaged by such verbal objectification. The engagement that excites him is the engagement with the whites, who have so suffocatingly circumscribed his life. Having revived the plan to rob Blum's Delicatessen, Bigger feels released from the numbed and half-dead existence that is normality to him.

> All that morning he had lurked behind his curtain of indifference and looked at things, snapping and glaring at whatever had tried to make him come out into the open. But now he was out; the thought of the job at Blum's and the tilt he had had with Gus had snarled him into things and his self-trust was gone. Confidence could only come again now through action so violent that it would make him forget.

The fear of the whites threatens Bigger's sense of manly self-control. Amongst the gang it is that fear which creates a brutal community. Bigger humiliates Gus, forcing him to lick the tip of Bigger's knife, in order to prevent the gang from carrying out the planned armed robbery of Blum's. He knew that "the fear of robbing a white man had had hold of him when he started the fight with Gus." But, as this is a knowledge too costly to be admitted, Bigger's psyche represses it. "He knew it in a way that kept it from coming to his mind in the form of a hard and sharp idea. . . . But he kept this knowledge of his thrust firmly down in him: his courage to live depended upon how successfully his fear was hidden from his consciousness."

This attitude on Bigger's part, this holding his own consciousness at arm's length, is perhaps Wright's most original achievement in his characterization of Bigger. Unlike his creator, Bigger has, as his story opens, almost no access to his own symbolic imagination, his own creative consciousness. His almost formalized imaginative act is the role-playing game he engages Gus in—"playing white." The roles—general, banker, President—are satiric (and thus aggressive) but they are quickly abandoned when their nasty double edge is felt: the absurd pomposity and venality of the powerful whites control the boys' imaginations even in parody. Bigger has never experienced the fulfillment Wright got from the act of writing, that Jamesian sense of an invigorating self-integration and self-satisfaction that is the hallmark of a stable identity. In Francis Fergusson's terminology, the central "action" of the novel, dictated by Bigger's "purpose" in this story, is "to discover an identity." The search for the murderer that occupies the Daltons, the police, and the reporters, the search for motives and evidence by the attorneys, the search for a mode of acquittal by Max are all counterpointed with Bigger's increasingly conscious search for an integrated and satisfying consciousness of who he is.

This important aspect of Wright's exclusive use of Bigger's point of view has been at the center of the critical contention surrounding the novel's achievement. Some, like John Bayliss, see Bigger as merely pathetic in his struggles with consciousness, slow-witted and environmentally unsuited for urban society. More astute critics characteristically lose track of the fact that it is Bigger's point of view we are dealing with, and begin to attribute what Fergusson would call "the movement of the spirit" in the novel entirely to the author's, and not the character's, psyche. Thus Robert Bone notes that Wright succeeds in balancing the "stark horror" of the story with the "spiritual anguish" promised in the novel's epigraph from the Book of Job—"Even today is my complaint rebellious; my stroke is heavier than my groaning"—but he finally sees this anguish in terms of Wright rather than Bigger:

> This note of anguish, which emphasizes Bigger's suffering, is so intense as to be almost physical in character. It is sustained by a style which can only be called visceral. The author writes from his guts, describing the emotional state of his characters in graphic psychosomatic terms. It is a characteristic device which has its source in Wright's aching memory of the deep south.
>
> (*The Negro Novel in America*)

The observation, as this essay attempts to demonstrate, is essentially true. But it is no less true that the critic here—and later in his essay as well—refuses to deal with the nature of Bigger's individuality as it comes to grips with itself. He winds up summing the novel's themes thus: "Bigger is a human being whose environment has made him incapable of relating meaningfully to other human beings except through murder." Surely this does not give much room to that "movement of the spirit" which Wright's epigraph from Scripture suggests we should seek. Donald Gibson has addressed himself to this curious obtuseness of critics who fail to deal with the totality of the character, charging them with sociocultural blindness: "most critics of Wright's novel see only the outer covering of Bigger Thomas, the blackness of his skin and his resulting social role. Few have seen him as a discrete entity, a particular person, who struggles with the burden of his humanity."

Considered as more than a representative figure or pawn in a sociological murder-melodrama, Bigger's story extends from the brilliantly epitomic opening domestic scene to his dismissal of Max on the last page of the narrative, and not, as many of Gibson's "blind" readers would have it, from Mary Dalton's murder to Boris Max's defense. Bigger's purpose, the action which this novel imitates, is the search for identity, an identity denied him by both his social milieu and his family situation. Bigger seeks a world in which he is not an alienated being, a world in which he can be "at home." Bigger's severe alienation from his human environments is matched by a sensual awareness (expressed in what Bone calls Wright's "visceral" prose style) which develops a nearly philosophical intensity. Thus, Wright manages to replicate, through the experience of Bigger, his own experience in coming to terms with his imagination as the "at home" identity that would save him from the familial and social threat that surrounded him. In Bigger's case it is not a mediated and formalized form of aggression that is the instrument of liberation, but rather the unmediated, literal, and violent murders of Mary Dalton and Bessie Mears.

Given the conflict that characterized Wright's relationship with his family womenfolk, it is, of course, highly significant that both of Bigger's victims are women. It is perhaps a more significant fact that one is white, the other black. In Wright's short stories the black men were victims and the women either bystanders and supporters or burdens and betrayers. The image of black woman as heroine and Communist in "Bright and Morning Star" was an afterthought, an anomaly. In Native Son, with its central image of the black man in rebellion against the victimizing strictures and constraints that retard his development, the targets of the attack are women.

Now Wright's difficulties with women were not, of course, limited to childhood traumas and adolescent misunderstandings of motive. He gave the name "Mary Dalton" to Bigger's first victim at least in part because it was the "nom de guerre" of a Communist Party member in Chicago whom Wright disliked intensely. More importantly, at the time he was writing Native Son, Wright's sexual relationships with women had begun to reflect and fulfill the patterns that had been established in his new home life.

After moving to New York in 1937, Wright lived for a time with the Sawyers, a modest black family, on 143rd Street in Harlem. Wright became sexually involved with the daughter of the household, Marian Sawyer, and their engagement was announced in the spring of 1938. Early in May, Wright rushed into the apartment of his friends, the Newtons, "announcing that according to the prenuptial physical examination Marian had an advanced case of syphilis." Feeling "outraged that he had been deceived and relieved that he had escaped from such a grave danger," Wright immediately broke with the Sawyers and moved into the Newtons' new apartment in Brooklyn (Michel Fabre, *The Unfinished Quest of Richard Wright*).

Jane Newton quickly became a significant literary confidante; Wright read to her from his manuscript and respected her suggestions for changes. Before completing the novel (in early June of 1939), he had seriously courted two more women, both white. When Ellen Poplar hesitated to commit herself to a marriage within a month or so, Wright married Dhima Rose Meadman "at the beginning of August 1939, in the sacristy of the Episcopal Church on Covenant Avenue, with Ralph Ellison as best man" (Fabre).

In the Marian Sawyer affair Wright can only have felt betrayed and nearly trapped by the sexual connection. Her illness, "advanced" or not, could only serve—as his mother's illness, so recently escaped—to limit or divert him. The whole business revived in him the sense of threat posed by women, a sense of threat deeply ingrained in him at home. A marriage, contracted in large part, it seems (judging by the precipitous and absolute rupture between the couple), on Wright's conventional sense of guilt and responsibility for the illicit sexual contact, is avoided when the woman is proven a "betrayer," threatening Wright with disease, disgrace, and/or the misery and limitation of continued guilt-ridden nursing duties. In the marriage, Wright seems to have been reacting rather than acting. The evidence suggests that while Dhima Rose Meadman was attractive to Wright, his strongest reason for marrying her was the apparent rejection of his proposal by Ellen Poplar. After an unhappy season in Mexico, Wright and Dhima separated and divorced. Fabre indicates that Wright "had never stopped blaming himself for his impatience and injustice" toward Ellen, and when they met at the Newtons' late in 1940 their union was quickly sealed. Benefit of clergy was bestowed in March 1941, after which the Wrights moved out of the Newtons' apartment and set up housekeeping on their own. Ellen Poplar's hesitation was a challenge to Wright's ego; the marriage to Dhima was his response, a demonstration of his independence and self-sufficiency, his worthiness and adequacy.

Wright felt a strong resentment of his need for sexual and human companionship from women. After the publication of *Native Son*, he engaged in an experiment with Frederic Wertham, a psychoanalyst, to discover whether there were any direct associations of Bigger's murder of Mary in Wright's background. Wertham and Wright probed for some connections between Wright's experience in white households in the South during his youth and the key scene of Bigger's smothering Mary in the presence of her blind mother. Wright began to recall working for a young couple who lived with the wife's mother when he was about fifteen years old. The woman was very friendly to Wright, "and he felt this was a second home to him." He tended the fireplace, lighting the day's heat on winter mornings. One morning he opened a door in the course of these duties to discover the young woman partly dressed; he was reprimanded and told to knock.

As a careful reading of *Black Boy* makes clear, in Wright's life the ego ideal derived from the mother and not the father. And Wertham notes that "the very symbol of the seeing eye that is blind fits the mother image." By extension, of course, all the blind, questing authorities in *Native Son*, who seek to punish Bigger for his transgressions against the two women, are derived from Wright's own mother. In the experience explored with Wertham, the patterns of response to female authority, sexuality, and affection which had been set at home, made themselves manifest in a situation that was also socially charged with threat: even at fifteen, Wright knew the danger of being accused of sexual improprieties with a white woman.

In the novel, the "outering" of these conflict patterns in the life of Bigger Thomas is more complex, I believe, than Wertham and Wright's little experiment demonstrated. For in considering the total action of *Native Son*—the psychic motive out of which the events are generated—as Bigger's effort "to discover an identity," the killing of white Mary Dalton, half-accidental and unconscious as it is, is secondary to the purposeful and free act of killing black Bessie Mears.

Mary Dalton's death is Dreiserian, determined by Bigger's social conditioning and the terrible pressure of the moment. Mary's clumsy efforts at social egalitarianism and Marxist comraderie with her father's new chauffeur make only for confusion in Bigger's mind. He recoils from their attempts at intimacy, for it sharpens his shame and hatred of his status.

> He felt he had no physical existence at all right then: he was something he hated, the badge of shame which he knew was attached to a black skin. It was a shadowy region, a No

Man's Land, the ground that separated the white world
from the black that he stood upon. He felt naked, transparent; he felt that this white man (Jan Erlone), having
helped to put him down, having helped to deform him, held
him up now to look at him and be amused. At that moment he
felt toward Mary and Jan a dumb, cold, and inarticulate hate.

Bigger feels vividly his condition of being "cut dead" by his social
environment; Jan's and Mary's efforts at being friendly only exacer-
bate and intensify Bigger's sense of shame, fear, and hatred. The unreal,
dreamlike quality of the murder scene later, comes into the tone of the
novel here, with Bigger's uncomfortable journey across the city in the
car, squeezed between Jan and Mary, who are completely blind to his
terror. After the killing, Bigger realizes the absurdity: "It all seemed
foolish! He wanted to laugh. It was unreal. He had to lift a dead woman
and he was afraid. He felt that he had been dreaming of something like
this for a long time, and then, suddenly, it was true."

Killing Mary is thus clearly, for Bigger, a release of long pent-
up aggressive tendencies that are both sexual and social. The act opens
Bigger to a flood of realizations that he had managed all his life to
repress with a half-conscious resistance. His vision cleared by his
irreversible act, Bigger comes to grasp the essential blindness of both
black and familial authority and white social authority. Having already grasped blind Mrs. Dalton's similarity to his mother and re-
sponded to it in kind, Bigger now sees that his own mother moves
like a blind person, "touching objects with her fingers as she passed
them, using them for support."

Bigger is elated by this perception of the essential blindness of all
those who would censor and punish him for the as yet undiscovered
murder. "His being black and at the bottom of the world was something which he could take with a new born strength. What his knife
and gun had once meant to him, his knowledge of having secretly
murdered Mary now meant." But this sense of power does not satisfy
him. Bigger finds that he wants to tell the world what he has done:

He wanted the keen thrill of startling them. . . . He wished
that he could be an image in their minds; that his black face
and the image of his smothering Mary and cutting off her
head and burning her could hover before their eyes as a
terrible picture of reality which they could see and feel and
yet not destroy.

Bigger's sense of his act of murder as a creative expression, as an act which confers on him a meaningful identity in his own eyes, is incomplete, even though "the knowledge that he had killed a white girl they loved and regarded as their symbol of beauty made him feel the equal of them, like a man who had been somehow cheated, but had now evened the score." Something more is required. Full psychic liberation can come to Bigger only when the image of his self reflected back at him by others coincides with his own image of his self. Although the knowledge of having murdered Mary Dalton replaces in his mind the sense of security that carrying a knife and a gun had given him,

> he was not satisfied with the way things stood now; he was a man who had come in sight of a goal, then had won it, and in winning it had seen just within his grasp another goal, higher, greater. He had learned to shout and had shouted and no ear had heard him; he had just learned to walk and was walking but could not see the ground beneath his feet; and had long been yearning for weapons to hold in his hands and suddenly found that his hands held weapons that were invisible.

Charles James has pointed out that Bigger's girl, Bessie, "is the ear he needs to sound out the meaning of Mary's death. Through her, Bigger can gain some insight into his family's judgement of his act, without actually telling them." For Bessie is an oasis of motherly comfort in Bigger's world. Wright presents her and their essentially physical relationship in pastoral terms infused with stock female symbols—the "Fallow field" and "the warm night sea" and the cooling and cleansing "fountain" whose "warm waters" cleared Bigger's senses "to end the tiredness and to reforge in him a new sense of time and space." This passive, maternal, all-accepting and sensually refreshing aspect of his mistress contrasts strongly in Bigger's mind with "the other Bessie," the questioning and censoring aspect of her which arouses in Bigger a desire "to clench his fist and swing his arm and blot out, kill, sweep away" all her resistance to his will and ideas.

Bessie's failure to understand and endorse the meaning Bigger has found in killing Mary Dalton dooms her. When Bigger tells her what he has done, she is terrified that she will be implicated. Her near-hysterical outburst of weak fatalism contains an explicit rejection of Bigger's very being—"I wish to God I never seen you. I wish one of us had died before we was born"—and makes Bigger realize that she can neither accompany him on his flight, nor be left behind to betray him. Bessie has proven herself to be like his mother: weak, limited, blind. "He hated his mother for that way of hers that was like Bessie's. What his mother had was Bessie's whiskey, and Bessie's whiskey was his mother's religion." Bigger begins to conceive of killing Bessie as a free act, "as a man seeing what he must do to save himself and feeling resolved to do it."

Killing Bessie, Bigger comes closer than in killing Mary to direct expression of Richard Wright's own primary inner conflict, the desire to strike out against the women who limited, repressed, censored, and punished his rebellious initiatives. Having killed Bessie with a brick, Bigger feels at last "truly and deeply" free and alive. The killings have given him a sense of freedom, and he is now able to make a direct contact with that consciousness he had for so long held at arm's length: "he had killed twice, but in a true sense it was not the first time he had ever killed. He had killed many times before, but only during the last two days had this impulse assumed the form of actual killing." His elation now is larger than the pride and sense of power he derived from killing Mary. This time, with this murder, he is brought to the brink of a philosophical consideration of his identity. As Charles James provocatively puts it, having "symbolically 'wiped out' the progenitive elements of the two things he hates most [the white societal oppressor and the black, submissive oppressed]," Bigger is free to begin thinking as an existentially liberated person:

> But what was he after? What did he want? What did he love and what did he hate? He did not know. There was something he *knew* and something he *felt*; something the *world* gave him and something he *himself* had; something spread out in *front* of him and something spread out in *back*; and never in all his life, with this black skin of his, had the two worlds, thought and feeling, will and mind, aspiration and satisfaction, been together; never had he felt a sense of wholeness.

Killing Bessie Mears puts Bigger in the position of a questor, consciously searching for an identity—"a sense of wholeness"— that will enable him to "be at home" in his society, "to be a part of the world, to lose himself in it so he could find himself, to be allowed a chance to live like others, even though he was black." From this point forward no other action has greater meaning. After the newspaper headlines announce "AUTHORITIES HINT SEX CRIMES," Bigger feels alienation settle down around him again: "Those words excluded him utterly from the world." He knows now that the meaning of his acts will be denied by the whites in their blind fury to capture and kill him. The accusation of sexual violation denies the individuality of his action, "cuts him dead" again. He knows that white society will refuse to see and confirm his new sense of identity, his real self, which he created by murdering Mary and Bessie, the dual images of his psychosocial oppression. Murdering Bessie, Charles James argues, "is Bigger's acknowledgement of his own impending death. He knows he must be caught, so from that moment his energy is devoted to salvaging 'spiritual victory.' "

The ambiguity of Mary Dalton's death required, for Wright's satisfaction, an unambiguous and legitimate murder, for which Bigger can confess and be punished. Lest he again create a story that bankers' daughters might tearfully enjoy, he wedded the American, Dreiserian naturalist tradition and the Russian, Dostoevskian existential tradition to make Bigger's passion for murder as broadly meaningful as possible. Against the resistance of his friend Jane Newton to his plan for killing off Bessie, Wright was adamant: "But I have to get rid of her. She must die!" he insisted (Fabre). Killing Bessie was thus an act of self-liberation for Wright as well as for Bigger. At the very least,

> Bigger's murder of Bessie marked a new stage in Wright's literary evolution: everything that he had learned from his naturalist models up to this point had prevented him from allowing his characters to give in to these demonic temptations, but now Bigger claimed his right to "create" in the existentialist meaning of the word, by rejecting the accidental nature of his first murder with this further proof of his power to destroy.
>
> (Michel Fabre, The Unfinished Quest of Richard Wright)

But more than this, I think, can be ventured. Wright's conception of Bigger as existential killer, forging out of the violence in his psyche a desperate and necessary identity, served also to manifest what Daniel Aaron calls "his hidden and perhaps repressed opposition to the Party." Wright's intense concern with Bigger's psychological motives and existential plight were not the flowerings of his Marxist perspective. Wright, as Aaron suggests, was leading a sort of intellectual double life:

> One side of him—the Black Marxist, very likely a true believer in the Party's fight against its enemies at home and abroad—contributed useful articles and poems and stories to the Party press. The other and private side tried to explain and define the meaning of being Black in white America, tried to discover his own identity and in effect, to create himself.

Wright's "private" perspective fostered his insistence on the personal, psychological dimensions of the black experience, and brought him, inevitably, into conflict with the essentially pamphleteering approach of the American Communists.

In a letter to Mike Gold, written shortly after Gold's defense of *Native Son* in the *Daily Worker* of April 29, 1940, Wright attacked the simplistic agitprop and proletarian-heroes-vs.-capitalist-villains mentality of many in the Party:

> An assumption which says that a Communist writer must follow well established lines of perception and feeling, must deal with that which is readily recognizable and typical, must depict reality only in terms of how it looks from a common and collective plane of reality . . . might seem sound. But I think those who put forward this reasoning forget the international framework in which we live and struggle today. . . . Are we Communist writers to be confined merely to the political and economic spheres of reality and leave the dark and hidden places of the human personality to the Hitlers and the Goebbels? I refuse to believe such. . . . Not to plunge into the complex jungle of human relationships and analyze them is to leave the field to the fascists and I won't and can't do that.

This vehement dissent from Party tradition, if not doctrine, was the beginning of Wright's dissociation from the Communists. He had found a supportive community amongst them, and through that community had found friends and a wife. But now the Party too had become a limiting and censoring authority in his life. His Communist readers were puzzled and displeased with his creation, Bigger Thomas. In the same letter to Gold, Fabre reports, "Wright complained that

Bigger's humanity, so obvious to him, meant so little to them, and that Ben David [a prominent and powerful black Communist] thought Max should have pleaded 'not guilty.' "

Part of the fault is Wright's, for his long interpolation of Max's sociological appeal, while it puts across a necessary ideological interpretation of Bigger's situation, nevertheless serves to distract the reader's attention from Bigger's strategies for dealing with his final days. Kenneth Burke has attempted to justify Wright's handling of Max by arguing that the lawyer's long address is a "conceptual epitome" of the novel's emotional themes, "a culmination of the book in the sense that an essayist's last chapter might recapitulate in brief the argument of his whole book." In Burke's view, Wright, "after the symbolic committing of the offences through his imaginative identification with Bigger, had thus ritualistically 'transcended' the offences. . . . His role as Marxist critic transcended his role as Negro novelist." As indebted as I am to Burke in general, I must disagree with him in this particular. Book 3 of *Native Son* is not a capstone, some neatly trimmed and tailored conclusion of a case study, but rather an open-ended or suspended argument in which Wright is refusing to allow Bigger's individuality to be swallowed up or subsumed by Max's social analyses.

When Bigger's crime career ends, and he is captured and brought bumpily down to earth, dragged by his ankles into the cold, white, enshrouding snow, he is forced to set aside the sense of power that the murders had given him. The motive which has impelled his behavior throughout, however—his drive to find a viable sense of identity—is not cast aside. It is in fact now his only concern. In the face of his impending death he must come to terms with his life, find some way to accept it, if he is to be "at home" in the world before he leaves it forever. The release of his repressive tension in the acts of murder was not useless; as in a dream, Bigger's expression of his internalized, repressed aggression makes subconscious data available to his conscious mind. As Bigger considers his end, then, the complex social considerations of Max's argument do not figure in his thought. Max's elaborate analogies and metaphors are lost on Bigger. The materials of Bigger's final meditations are his own perceptions of the world around him, freed from stereotype and threat by his murderous acts. The structure of book 3 is provided by Bigger's efforts to realize out of these materials a vision of social relatedness, a sense of his being and belonging in the world. He asks:

If he reached out his hands, and if his hands were electric wires, and if his heart were a battery giving life and fire to those hands, and if he reached out with his hands and touched other people, if he did that, would there be a reply, a shock?

And in seeking an answer Bigger rejects the alternatives his life had presented to him. As Robert Bone notes, "He rejects his family ('Go home, Ma.'); his fellow prisoners ('Are you the guy who pulled the Dalton job?'); the race leaders ('They almost like white folks when it comes to guys like me.') and religion." His spiritual victory, if he is to have one, must come from within, be composed entirely of the stuff of the self. "He was balanced on a hairline now, but there was no one to push him forward or backward, no one to make him feel that he had any value or worth—no one but himself."

Bigger comes through to a sense of identification with a human community at the very conclusion of his life and story. In his last conversation with Max, Bigger is calm and composed. Max has come "to offer compassion when Bigger seeks meaning," but "Bigger takes control of that final interview and 'comforts' Max" (Charles L. James). Max tries to give Bigger hope in a future collective human salvation, a Marxist vision of men reclaiming the world from their bosses. Bigger takes from what Max says confirmation of his new inner feeling, newly arrived at, that "at bottom all men lived as he had lived and felt as he had felt." Max tells him "the job in getting people to fight and have faith is in making them believe in what life has made them feel, making them feel that their feelings are as good as those of others." The feelings that Bigger accepts in himself are not, as so many critics have asserted, those of fear, shame, and hatred. But, Paul Siegel has recently noted, "it is hard to make men hear who will not listen. Seven times in the last page and a half of the novel Bigger cries out to Max, 'I'm all right,' the last time adding, 'For real, I am.' " Bigger is all right because, as he tries to tell Max, when he thinks about what Max has said he feels that he was right for wanting what he wanted—a sense of human integration, wholeness, identity.

> "They wouldn't let me live and I killed. Maybe it ain't fair to kill, and I reckon I really didn't want to kill. But when I think of why all the killing was, I begin to feel what I wanted, what I am. . . . I didn't want to kill! . . . But what I killed for, I *am*! It must've been pretty deep in me to make

me kill! . . . What I killed for must've been good. . . . I
didn't know I was really alive in this world until I felt things
hard enough to kill for 'em."

Now Siegel is too busy defending Max to take note of the fact
that Bigger is not defending his hate and shame but rather the motive
that lay behind all the actions of his short life—the unsatisfied drive
to reject the negative identity that the cultural stereotypes had forced
on him and to discover an adequate, integral replacement. Max, for
all his good will, has never really seen Bigger's individual humanity.
As Donald Gibson notes, he "cannot accept the implications of
Bigger's conclusions, nor indeed, can he fully understand the
position that Bigger has finally arrived at." As he departs Max
gropes for his hat, "like a blind man." At the last Bigger speaks as a
free man and equal human being not to Max, who can not, finally,
look him in the eye, but to Jan. Jan has paid his dues, suffered, and
learned to see Bigger as a human being.

IV

At least implicitly, then, *Native Son* denies the notion of human
salvation and integration through the medium of social process, even
radical social process. Max, as spokesman for the political and social
left, is unable either to give Bigger a satisfying ideological social
vision or to measure the angle of vision from which Bigger views the
world. Wright's separation from the Communist view of reality is
foreshadowed here in the image of failed contact between Max and
Bigger. If in Bigger's murderous rage Wright was elaborating
personal as well as intellectual and social aggression, then in Bigger's
rejection of Max's view of reality as inadequate Wright was repudi-
ating the masked authority of the Party. Deep down, Wright felt a
continuing and unbridgeable alienation from family and society,
from religion, custom, and community. The Party had, for a time,
given him the support he needed to articulate, albeit in symbolic
terms, the elements of his situation. The symbolic outering of inner
conflicts that reached back into personal and familial history reduced
the pressure within and enabled him to marry and to carry on a
career, but it also made clearer to him the essential loneliness
incumbent on an person who, for whatever reason, must create a
sense of values for himself.

On Reading *Native Son*

David Bradley

I first began *Native Son* in Philadelphia, in the winter of 1971, when I was an undergraduate at the University of Pennsylvania and taking a course called "Readings in Black Literature." I had recently abandoned my major in English and invented a major in "Creative Writing," a course which I hoped would allow me to master the writer's craft while at the same time producing a novel good enough to convince a faculty committee that I should get a degree. The problem was that I wasn't sure that anybody around—myself included—knew what a good novel, in my case, was. The cause of that uncertainty was the concept of the black, or Afro-American, aesthetic.

The concept had been the subject of debate in black intellectual circles for almost a century, but in the late sixties and early seventies the idea that the art of black people ought to be created and judged by different principles and standards from the art of white people had become an article of faith. One formulation of this notion, very much in vogue at the University of Pennsylvania, had been articulated by James T. Stewart, a Philadelphia musician, in a 1966 essay, "The Development of the Black Revolutionary Artist." "The dilemma of the 'negro' artist," Stewart had written, "is that he makes assumptions based on . . . white models. These assumptions are not only wrong, they are even antithetical to his existence." Stewart went on to say that "[the black artist] must . . . be estranged from the dominant culture. . . . This means that he cannot be 'successful' in any sense that has meaning in white critical evaluations. Nor can his work ever be called 'good' in any context or meaning that could make sense to that traditional critique. . . . 'Ineptitude' and 'unfitness' will be an aspect of what we do."

My dilemma was that at the University of Pennsylvania white definitions of "ineptitude" and "unfitness" were rigorously applied; if Stewart was right, I was going to have a hard time becoming a black writer while also getting a degree. On the other hand, I might already be a black writer, my brilliance unrecognized because my work was being judged by inappropriate standards. I took "Black Literature" hoping to discover I was already a good writer and, if not, how to become one by reading what everybody seemed to agree were the classics of my people. One of these, of course, was *Native Son*.

Although I had never read *Native Son*, I had long been aware of it. In the politically charged atmosphere of a late-sixties campus, any black who wanted to be taken seriously by fellow blacks and/or liberal whites had to be able to invoke the names of black artists and scholars and the titles of their works whenever it was appropriate—and sometimes when it was not. And, since I had been an English major, I had occasionally run across references to *Native Son*; I knew, for example, of Irving Howe's declaration that "the day *Native Son* appeared, American culture was changed forever," and I had seen the contents page of David Littlejohn's *Black on White: A Critical Survey of Writing by American Negroes*, which had sections headed "Before *Native Son*: The Dark Ages" and "Before *Native Son*: The Renaissance and After." Also, since I wanted to be a writer but preferred not to starve, I was acutely aware that *Native Son* was the first book published in America to make a black author a lot of money. I therefore opened it with great expectations. And, like Dickens's Pip, I was terribly disappointed.

Put simply, I hated *Native Son*. Put more accurately, I hated it with a passion. Hated it because, while it had its artistic moments, it violated most of the principles of novelistic construction that I was struggling to master. The plot was improbable, the narrative voice intrusive, the language often stilted, and the characters, especially that silly little rich white tease Mary Dalton and her stupid, gigolo Communist boyfriend, Jan, were stereotypical beyond belief. At first I tried to rationalize these flaws as James T. Stewart's "ineptitude" and "unfitness," but I couldn't get around what I hated with a passion: Bigger Thomas.

It wasn't that Bigger failed as a character, exactly. I had read the novel's prefatory material, which, in the edition my class was using, was Wright's essay, "How 'Bigger' Was Born." I therefore knew that Wright had set out to write a book "no one would weep over." In this, for me, Wright succeeded; I shed no tears for Bigger, I wanted him dead, by legal means if possible, by lynching if necessary. (In fact, the only difference between me and the mob that pursued him was that I wanted him dead not for his accidental killing of Mary—I *understood* that, and would have preferred it to have been intentional—but for his intentional murder of Bessie, the black woman who loved him and would have done anything for him.) But I knew too that Wright had intended Bigger to be a flat character, so he could serve as a "meaningful and prophetic symbol" of the black masses. In this, for me, Wright failed—I did not see Bigger Thomas as a symbol of any kind of black man; to me he was a sociopath, pure and simple, beyond sympathy or understanding. In fact, I stopped reading *Native Son* at the point where Bigger, after practically raping Bessie, bashing her face in with a brick, and tossing her body down an airshaft, thinks that "he was living, truly and deeply." This, I thought, is sick.

I said so in class. I felt guilty about it, because all my life I had been schooled never to say a mumblin' word about any Negro whom the non-Negro world recognized as an achiever, which surely meant Richard Wright. I felt politically incorrect too, and so silently endured the charge, leveled by my politically correct classmates, that I had been so brainwashed by the dominant white culture that I was "not black enough" to appreciate *Native Son*. I did not even protest (although I thought about it) that it was the voices of dominant white culture which, as much as any, had declared *Native Son* a work of brilliance. I kept my mouth shut because my heresy went beyond *Native Son*. I hated the idea of Black Literature too, and was resolved that if the price of becoming a black writer was following the model of *Native Son*, I would just have to write like a honky. Fortunately, I found in works by other blacks—Charles Chesnutt, Jean Toomer, Zora Neale Hurston—reason to soften that stand. Still, reading *Native Son* turned me into an Afro-American pre-Raphaelite, determined that those models I took from black letters would come from Littlejohn's "Dark Ages," the days before *Native Son* changed America and made Richard Wright a lot of money.

I first finished *Native Son* in London, in the fall of 1973, when I was a graduate student at the University of London, ostensibly doing research for a thesis on the relationship between American history and the writing of American blacks. I say "ostensibly" because I was actually trying to maintain my emotional well-being in the face of various brands of English "racialism"—the generic bigotry of the English people (who were less than thrilled when the Empire became the Commonwealth and a lot of West Indian, African, and Asian former-colonials came to Mother England looking for jobs), the trademarked bigotry of my instructors (my principle tutor had published the statement that American black writers were "freaks"), and the homemade bigotry of my English fellow students, who asked ingenuous questions about rats, roaches, and Martin Luther King (with whom, they assumed, I'd dined regularly)—by hiding out in the British Museum, reading the essays of James Baldwin. Some of the essays, of course, were about *Native Son*.

Baldwin's essays expressed eloquently the ideas I had choked out in my Black Literature class. In "Everybody's Protest Novel" he upheld my aesthetics, charging that works belonging to that subgenre known as the protest novel, such as Harriet Beecher Stowe's *Uncle Tom's Cabin* and *Native Son*, were unreasonably forgiven "whatever violence they do to language, whatever excessive demands they make of credibility. It is, indeed, considered the sign of a frivolity so intense as to approach decadence to suggest that these books are badly written and wildly improbable." In "Many Thousands Gone" he criticized *Native Son* in particular: "A necessary dimension," Baldwin wrote, "has been cut away; this dimension being the relationship that Negroes bear to one another. . . . It is this which creates [the novel's] climate of anarchy and unmotivated and unapprehended disaster; and it is this climate . . . which has led us all to believe that in Negro life there exists no tradition, no field of manners, no possibility of ritual or intercourse." Aha! I thought triumphantly, let's see 'em tell James Baldwin *he* isn't black enough.

But Baldwin did something far more significant than rescue my claim to racial identity: in arguing that the flaws in *Native Son* were common to a group of novels distinguished not by the race of the author but by the form of the work, Baldwin was, in effect, challenging the black aesthetic. This made me realize that, although a course in Black Literature had made it possible for me to read works by black writers, which were otherwise absent from the curriculum, the assumptions behind the course had made it impossible for me to see those works—including *Native Son*—as part of an American, as opposed to an Afro-American, literary tradition. I wondered if I would have a different reaction to *Native Son* if I considered it in this new context. So I went in search of a copy.

My reaction was indeed different. Put simply, *Native Son* infuriated me. Put more sequentially, it bemused, astonished, horrified, and then infuriated me. And then it frightened me out of my wits.

The British Museum, as one might expect, had a copy of *Native Son*'s original edition, which included an introduction by Dorothy Canfield. That there was any introduction seemed curious; I couldn't see why a contemporary novel would require an introduction. Especially *that* introduction. For while Miss Canfield said the things you would expect an introducer to say, testifying that "the author shows genuine literary skill in the construction of his novel," and comparing him to Dostoevsky, she also said the things you would expect an introducer to scrupulously *not* say—for example, assuring readers that she "did not at all mean to imply that *Native Son* as literature is comparable to the masterpieces of Dostoievski." What was horrifying was what Miss Canfield thought *Native Son was* comparable to: "How to produce neuroses in sheep and psychopathic upsets in rats and other animals has been known to research scientists for so long that accounts of these experiments have filtered out to us, the general public." Miss Canfield began, and went on to state that "our society puts Negro youth in the situation of the animal in the psychological laboratory in which a neurosis is to be caused." *Native Son*, she said, was "the first report in fiction we have had from those who succumb to these distracting cross-currents of contradictory nerve impulses, from those whose behavior patterns give evidence of the same bewildered, senseless tangle of abnormal nerve-reactions studied in animals by psychologists in laboratory experiments."

Suddenly I realized that many of *Native Son*'s white readers *had* seen Bigger Thomas as a symbol of what black people were *really* like; things being what they were in 1940, when *Native Son* hit the shelves, they, like Mary Dalton, had probably never come into contact with enough blacks to know better. God, I thought in fury, they believed we were *all* Biggers. And, as I read on from the introduction to the novel itself, I found myself wondering how many of the attitudes of 1940s whites may have been confirmed, influenced, if not totally shaped by such a tremendously popular "report." Had *Native Son* contributed to the facts that, in 1942, less than half of all white Americans approved of integrated transportation facilities and that only around one in three approved of integrated schools or neighbor-hoods? And, if they found *Native Son* a credible "report," who could blame them for those attitudes? I myself did not want a nut like Bigger Thomas sitting next to me on a bus or in a schoolroom, and certainly I did not want him moving in next door. But, while Miss Canfield's infuriating ideas may have been accepted by the general public, it seemed incredible to me that the literary critics would also have accepted the characterization of a novel by Dostoevsky *or* Wright as a lab report. So I sought out Irving Howe's essay "Black Boys and Native Sons," from which the "changed the world" quote had come.

What I discovered was that Howe was as bad as Miss Canfield. True, he praised *Native Son* for having changed American culture, but he also wrote of "all its crudeness, melodrama and claustrophobia of vision. *Native Son* has grave faults [as] anyone can see. The language is often course, flat in rhythm, syntactically overburdened, heavy with journalistic slag." He compared Wright to Theodore Dreiser, but, like Miss Canfield, rushed to assure his readers that the compar-ison was limited and "finally of limited value, for the disconcerting reason that Dreiser had a white skin and Wright a black one. *Native Son*, though preserving some of the devices of the naturalistic novel, deviates sharply from its characteristic tone: a tone Wright could not possibly have maintained and which, it may be, no Negro novelist can really hold for long."

At that moment I saw how *Native Son* could be a classic according to the black aesthetic and still be loved by the white critics; the whites did not really view it as literature—except in the sense that scientific journals or polemical pamphlets are literature, writing of which one might say, "the style is terrible, but the data is fascinating." And I saw too how unmarked and treacherous was the road I would have to travel, when and if I did become a writer. I could not assume I was writing well if white critics praised my work *or* if they slammed it for "ineptitude" and "unfitness." They might praise it to the skies while still finding it inept and unfit, for they might be thinking of me, not as a writer, but as a laboratory rat who was just slightly more articulate than his fellows.

I read *Native Son* for the third time in the summer of 1977. I was living in New York and trying to make my way as a freelance writer. By that time I had written a novel called *South Street*, which had been acclaimed as a "black novel," and that prompted a magazine editor to invite me to review a "new" book by Richard Wright—who had died in Paris in 1960 and had been promptly cremated, with a copy of his autobiography, *Black Boy*, at his side. The appearance of a new book by Wright was due not to reincarnation, but to *Black Boy*'s curious publication history.

Black Boy, published in March 1945 (and which, like *Native Son* was a Book-of-the-Month Club selection), told the story of Wright's youth in the oppressive South and his escape North with his head "full of a hazy notion that life could be lived with dignity, that the personalities of others should not be violated, that men should be able to confront other men without fear or shame." The book's huge success—four hundred thousand copies were sold within a few weeks—was perhaps due to the fact that Wright's escape, which conformed to the pattern of the "Great Migration" of blacks from the rural South to the urban North during the first third of the century, when coupled with his unique fame (except for Joe Louis and Jesse Owens, he was probably the best known black in America; Jackie Robinson's big league debut was over two years away), made *BlackBoy* the quintessential Afro-American success story.

But it hadn't been that when Wright completed it in 1943, calling it *American Hunger*. Then it had gone on to describe the conditions that focused Wright's "hazy notion" of Northern possibilities into the pessimistic beliefs that shaped *Native Son*—his near-starvation in the Chicago ghetto, his lonely drive toward self-education, his Kafka-esque involvement with the Communist Party. Sometime in the middle of 1944, however, Wright's editor, Edward C. Aswell, said he felt "the book would break much more logically with the departure from the South." Wright had originally told his agent, Paul Reynolds, Jr., "I don't think that there is much I will ever be able to do on this script . . . on the whole, the thing will have to stand as it is, for better or worse." Still, he agreed not only to the cut of almost a third of the manuscript, but also to alter the tone of what was published as *Black Boy* by adding five concluding pages that contained that hopeful "hazy notion." The deleted portion of *American Hunger*, although parts of it saw scattered exposure in the 1940s, remained essentially unpublished until 1977. This was the "book" I was asked to review.

My response to the *American Hunger* story mirrored my reactions to the British Museum's copy of *Native Son*: bemusement at anyone's suggesting that Wright—or anybody—should write an autobiography while only thirty-two, astonishment at the effrontery of asking that the text of that autobiography be truncated (who *dares* to tell a man when the facts of his experience cease to be logical?), horror at Wright's acquiescence and worse, cooperation. The fury came as I read *American Hunger*, which seemed to me to be a virtual rewriting of *Native Son*. What inspired that idea was not the many correspondences between Wright's history and Bigger's (birth in Mississippi, lack of formal education beyond grammar school, and residence in Chicago, to name a few) but the presence of another character who seemed to spring from *Native Son*'s pages—Bessie.

At one point Wright earned a living selling burial insurance in the Chicago ghetto, where, he wrote, "there were many comely black housewives who, trying desperately to keep up their insurance payments, were willing to make bargains to escape paying a ten-cent premium each week" (*American Hunger*). Wright made such a "bargain" with "an illiterate black child with a baby whose father she did not know." While Wright did not bash this woman's face in with a brick, he did once threaten to kill her. He laughed at her when she admired his ability to express himself with words, once told her she should be in a circus, and viewed her as a pure sex object. "I could not talk to her," he wrote. "Sex relations were the only relations she had ever had; no others were possible with her, so limited was her intelligence." Once, he wrote, "[I] stared at her and wondered just what a life like hers meant in the scheme of things, and I came to the conclusion that it meant absolutely nothing."

Black folks have a word for a man who could say or even think that about a woman whose bed he's shared: cold. And that was the image of Wright that came to me as I read *American Hunger* and when I went back to read *Black Boy*. In both books I could see Wright, the frigid intellectual, portraying black people as psychological "types"— and then damning them for a lack of humanity. In *Black Boy* he wrote of "the simple nakedness" of his father's life, "how fastened were his memories to a crude and raw past, how chained were his actions and emotions to the direct, animalistic impulses of his withering body. . . . From the white landowners above him there had not been handed to him a chance to learn the meaning of loyalty, of sentiment, of tradition. Joy was unknown to him as was despair." Of black people in general he wrote, "I used to mull over the strange absence of real kindness in Negroes, how unstable was our tenderness, how lacking in genuine passion we were, how void of great hope, how timid our joy, how bare our traditions, how hollow our memories, how lacking we were in those intangible sentiments that bind man to man, and how shallow was even our despair. . . . I saw that what had been taken for our emotional strength was our negative confusions, our flights, our fears, our frenzy under pressure." In those passages I heard echoes of *Native Son*, of Bigger's contemptuous opinion of his family "inarticulate and unconscious, making for living without thinking, making for peace and habit, making for a hope that blinded"; I even heard echoes of the chapter headings that outlined the course of Bigger Thomas's life: "Fear," "Flight," and "Fate." What made me furious was not the suspicion that *Native Son* was autobiographical—an artist has a right to draw his material from wherever he chooses—but that Wright had written it twice; the echoes had to be conscious. Wright had to know these statements were untrue. But he also knew they confirmed the view of blacks that prevailed in the very society he accused of oppression, for, in *American Hunger*, he wrote that "my reading in sociology had enabled me to discern many strange types of Negro characters." He also knew that part of *Native Son*'s tremendous popularity had been a result of its satisfying such sociological expectations; far from rejecting Dorothy Canfield's characterization of *Native Son* as "a report," Wright so embraced it that he suggested that her review for the Book-of-the-Month Club News be used as an introduction to *Black Boy*. Put kindly, it seemed to me that Wright was pandering to white expectations. Put bluntly, I thought Richard Wright had sold his people down the river.

But as I searched furiously through *American Hunger* for quotes to support that view, I saw something which in my quick outrage I had overlooked. After saying that the life of the woman with whom he made love "meant absolutely nothing," Wright went on: "And neither did my life mean anything." And the awful thought occurred to me: what if Richard Wright believed what he wrote? What then might be the meaning of *Native Son*?

My second full reading of *Native Son* filled me with a terrible sorrow. Not for Bigger Thomas—I still did not give a damn about him—but for Richard Wright. For when I read the passage in which Mary Dalton tells Bigger she had long wanted to enter a ghetto house "and just *see* how your people live," I heard the echo of Dorothy Canfield's introduction. And when I read the passage in which Jan tells Bigger that it was really okay that Bigger killed the woman he (Jan) loved, because "You thought you were settling something, or you wouldn't've killed," I heard Irving Howe's blithe waiver of the aesthetic standards that he, as a critic, *had* to hold dear. And when I saw Bigger reiterating that piece of dialectical insanity, at the very end of his life, I saw Richard Wright letting somebody tell him where *his* life logically ended.

And I realized that previously when I read *Native Son* I had done it the injustice to trying to fit it into *my* America, a place where, while a black person's right to human dignity was not exactly a given, it was a thesis that could at least be argued. But Richard Wright's America was a very different place, a place where a black who hoped to survive needed a sense of humility more than a sense of dignity, and where Bigger Thomas's story was no more melodramatic, crude, or claustrophobic than the times themselves. In Richard Wright's America a writer could take reports directly from the newspapers to write a book like *Native Son*, and was glad to have that book introduced by anybody, never mind how they characterized it. In Richard Wright's America a best-selling, financially independent novelist—if he was a Negro—could not lunch with his agent in a midtown Manhattan restaurant, could not live with other writers in Greenwich Village, could not buy a house there, could rent there only if he found a landlord willing to defy half the neighborhood. In Richard Wright's America a critically acclaimed, Guggenheim-award-winning Negro novelist, would hesitate to use the surnames of his agent and his editor in the dedication of a book because he was not sure they would want to be so closely associated with a black. And in Richard Wright's America a black boy who wanted to be a writer could remain tragically unaware of the writing of black people, could say, while explaining where his own characters had come from, that "association with white writers was the life preserver of my hope to depict Negro life in fiction, for my race possessed no fictional works . . . that went with a deep and fearless will down to the dark roots of life" ("How 'Bigger' Was Born"). In Richard Wright's America they didn't even have Black Literature courses.

Seeing that, I realized that *Native Son* was not as inaccurate as I had thought, and that, in a sense, Dorothy Canfield was not entirely wrong. Not that there was great validity in Wright's use of Bigger Thomas as a type—there are Biggers, but all black men are not he, nor does every black walk around with Bigger lurking in the corner of his mind. Nor is there validity in reading any piece of fiction as a "report" of general social conditions. But fiction is a report of specific conditions; that is its value. *Native Son*, I realized, shows the vision one black man held of his people, his country, and, ultimately, himself. Dear God, I thought, how horrible for a man to have to write this. And, please God, I thought, let no one ever have to write this again.

It is now the autumn of 1986. I have just finished reading *Native Son* for the fourth time. I have been invited to write an introduction to this new edition of *Native Son*, which the Book-of-the-Month Club is publishing as part of the Club's sixtieth anniversary commemoration. Put simply—and frighteningly, to me—I have been asked to step into the role of Dorothy Canfield Fisher, and dared to do a better job.

I am not sure I can do a better job. For while what Miss Canfield wrote still infuriates me, she was a part of her time, as I am a part of mine. Still, I have had the opportunity—as Miss Canfield did not—to read *Native Son* over a span of years. And I find that I can be kinder toward *Native Son* than I was in the past.

Not that I think *Native Son* has suddenly become artistically brilliant. But now I see its flaws in a way that was not possible because of all the baggage of criticism and politics it carried, and because I myself lacked the perspective a writer in time acquires. For one thing, I have belatedly realized that *Native Son* is a first novel. Its flaws are typical of first novels and are no more severe than those found in most. It ain't great, but it also ain't chopped liver. For another, I can see that *Native Son* is, in fact, a valuable and frightening document— not of sociology, but of history. It says to us that there was once a time in this land of freedom when a man could have such a bleak and frightening vision of his people and when we had so little contact with one another that that vision could be accepted as fact.

But despite that, I find that Wright, after all these years, has failed in an ironic way. He wanted *Native Son* to be a book "no one would weep over." With me, he once succeeded. He no longer does. I hope he will not with you. For my vision is that *Native Son* is an ineffably sad expression of what once were the realities of this nation. We have not come as far as we ought, but I hope we have come far enough now, to read *Native Son* and weep.

Chronology

1908	Richard Wright born to Ella and Nathan Wright on a farm outside Natchez, Mississippi.
1914	Nathan Wright deserts the family.
1916–25	Attends, with interruptions, public and Seventh-Day Adventist schools.
1924	Publishes "The Voodoo of Hell's Half-Acre" in the black *Southern Register*.
1925	Graduates as valedictorian from Smith-Robinson Public School; moves to Memphis.
1927–36	Works as a postal clerk in Chicago, where he becomes an active writer for leftist publications. He joins the John Reed Club and the Communist Party U.S.A.
1937	Becomes Harlem editor of the *Daily Worker*.
1938	*Uncle Tom's Children*, a collection of short stories, published.
1939	Receives Guggenheim Fellowship. Marries Dhima Rose Meadman.
1940	Publishes *Native Son*. Wright and Dhima are divorced.
1941	Marries Ellen Poplar. Works with Paul Green towards a stage version of *Native Son*. *Twelve Million Black Voices* published.
1942	Julia Wright born.
1945	Publishes *Black Boy*. Meets James Baldwin.
1946	Visits France.
1947	Moves to France, his home for the rest of his life.
1949	Rachel Wright born.
1949–50	Stays in Argentina, filming *Native Son*. Wright himself appears as Bigger.
1953	*The Outsider* published. Visits the Gold Coast (now Ghana).
1954	*Black Power* and *Savage Holiday* published. Visits Spain.

1955   Attends the Bandung Conference in Indonesia.

1956   *The Color Curtain: A Report on the Bandung Conference* and *Pagan Spain* published.

1957   *White Man, Listen!* published.

1958   *The Long Dream,* to be the first of a trilogy, published.

1960   Dies suddenly of heart failure during a hospital stay for an unrelated complaint. At the time of his death Wright was selecting the best of some thousands of his haiku for publication.

Contributors

HAROLD BLOOM, Sterling Professor of the Humanities at Yale University, is the author of *The Anxiety of Influence, Poetry and Repression*, and many other volumes of literary criticism. His forthcoming study, *Freud: Transference and Authority*, attempts a full-scale reading of all of Freud's major writings. A MacArthur Prize Fellow, he is general editor of five series of literary criticism published by Chelsea House. During 1987–88, he served as Charles Eliot Norton Professor of Poetry at Harvard University.

DAN McCALL, who taught literature at Cornell University, is the author of the novel *The Man Says Yes*.

ROGER ROSENBLATT, formerly literary editor of *The New Republic*, is the author of *Black Fiction*.

JOEL ROACHE teaches English at the University of Maryland, Eastern Shore.

MICHAEL G. COOKE is Professor of English at Yale University. His books include *Afro-American Literature in the Twentieth Century: The Achievement of Intimacy* and *Acts of Inclusion: Studies Bearing on an Elemental Theory of Romanticism*.

JOYCE ANN JOYCE teaches English at the University of Maryland, College Park. She is the author of *Richard Wright's Art of Tragedy*.

LOUIS TREMAINE is Assistant Professor of English at the University of Richmond, where he specializes in modern African literature.

VALERIE SMITH is Associate Professor of English at Princeton University. She is the author of *Self-Discovery and Authority in Afro-American Narrative*.

BARBARA JOHNSON is Professor of French and Comparative Literature at Harvard University. Her books include *The Critical Difference* and *World of Difference*.

JOSEPH T. SKERRETT, JR., is Associate Professor of English at the University of Massachusetts, Amherst. He has published widely on twentieth-century black fiction and psychobiography.

DAVID BRADLEY, the novelist, teaches writing at Temple University. He is the author of *South Street* and *The Chaneysville Incident*.

Bibliography

Abcarian, Richard. *Richard Wright's* Native Son: *A Critical Handbook.* Belmont, Calif.: Wadsworth, 1970.

Amis, Lola J. "Richard Wright's *Native Son*: Notes." *Negro American Literature Forum* 8 (1974): 240–43.

Avery, Evelyn Gross. *Rebels and Victims: The Fiction of Richard Wright and Bernard Malamud.* Washington, N.Y.: Kennikat, 1979.

Baker, Houston A., Jr. "Racial Wisdom and Richard Wright's *Native Son*." In *Long Black Song: Essays in Black American Literature and Culture*, 122–41. Charlottesville: University Press of Virginia, 1972.

———, ed. *Twentieth Century Interpretations of* Native Son. Englewood Cliffs, N.J.: Prentice-Hall, 1972.

Bakish, David. *Richard Wright.* New York: Ungar, 1973.

Baldwin, James. "Everybody's Protest Novel." *Partisan Review* 16 (1949): 578–85.

Baldwin, Richard E. "The Creative Vision of *Native Son*." *The Massachusetts Review* 14 (1973): 278–90.

Baron, Dennis E. "The Syntax of Perception in Richard Wright's *Native Son*." *Language and Style* 9 (1976): 17–28.

Bone, Robert A. *Richard Wright.* Minneapolis: University of Minnesota Press, 1969.

Boulton, H. Philip. "The Role of Paranoia in Richard Wright's *Native Son*." *Kansas Quarterly* 7, no. 3 (1975): 111–24.

Brazinsky, Judith Giblin. "The Demands of Conscience and the Imperatives of Form: The Dramatization of *Native Son*." *Black American Literature Forum* 18 (1984): 106–9.

Brignano, Russell C. *Richard Wright: An Introduction to the Man and His Works.* Pittsburgh: University of Pittsburgh Press, 1970.

Brivic, Sheldon. "Conflict of Values: Richard Wright's *Native Son*." *Novel* 7 (1974): 231–45.

Brown, Lloyd W. "Stereotypes in Black and White: The Nature of Perception in Wright's *Native Son*." *Black Academy Review* 1, no. 3 (1970): 35–44.

Brunette, Peter. "Two Wrights, One Wrong." In *The Modern American Novel and the Movies*, edited by Gerald Peary and Robert Shatzkin. New York: Ungar, 1978.

Bryant, Jerry H. "The Violence of *Native Son*." *The Southern Review* 17 (1981): 303–19.

Burgum, Edwin Berry. "The Promise of Democracy in Richard Wright's *Native Son*." In *The Novel and the World's Dilemmas*, 223–40. New York: Russell & Russell, 1963.

Butler, Robert James. "Wright's *Native Son* and Two Novels by Zola: A Comparative Study." *Black American Literature Forum* 18 (1984): 100–105.

Cauley, Anne O. "A Definition of Freedom in the Fiction of Richard Wright." *CLA Journal* 19 (1976): 327–46.

CLA Journal 12, no. 4 (1969). Special issue on Wright.

Clark, Beverly Lyon. "Bigger Thomas' Name." *North Dakota Quarterly* 47, no. 1 (1979): 80.

Cobb, Nina Kressner. "Richard Wright: Individualism Reconsidered." *CLA Journal* 21 (1978): 335–54.

Cooke, Michael G. *Afro-American Literature in the Twentieth Century: The Achievement of Intimacy.* New Haven: Yale University Press, 1984.

Creekmore, Herbert. "Social Factors in *Native Son*." *The University Review* 8 (1941): 136–43.

Cripps, Thomas. "*Native Son*." *New Letters* 38, no. 2 (1971): 49–63.

Davis, Charles T., and Michel Fabre. *Richard Wright: A Primary Bibliography.* Boston: G. K. Hall, 1982.

De Arman, Charles. "Bigger Thomas: The Symbolic Negro and the Discrete Human Entity." *Black American Literature Forum* 12 (1978): 61–64.

Demarest, David P., Jr. "Richard Wright: The Meaning of Violence." *Negro American Literature Forum* 8 (1974): 236–39.

Ellison, Ralph. "The World and the Jug." In *Shadow and Act*, 115–47. New York: Random House, 1953.

Emanuel, James A. "Fever and Feeling: Notes on the Imagery of *Native Son*." *Negro Digest* 18 (1968): 16–26.

Fabre, Michel. "Fantasies and Style in Richard Wright's Fiction." *New Letters* 46, no. 3 (1980): 55–81.

———. *The Unfinished Quest of Richard Wright.* Translated by Isabelle Barzun. New York: William Morrow, 1973.

Felgar, Robert. " 'The Kingdom of the Beast': The Landscape of *Native Son*." *CLA Journal* 17 (1974): 333–37.

———. *Richard Wright.* Boston: Twayne, 1980.

Fishburn, Katherine. *Richard Wright's Hero: The Faces of a Rebel-Victim.* Metuchen, N.J.: Scarecrow, 1977.

Fleissner, Robert. "How Bigger's Name Was Born." *Studies in Black Literature* 8, no.1 (1977): 4–5.

Fleming, Robert E. "O'Neill's *The Hairy Ape* as a Source for *Native Son*." *CLA Journal* 28 (1985): 434–43.

Gaffney, Kathleen. "Bigger Thomas in Richard Wright's *Native Son*." *Roots* 1, no. 1 (1970): 81–95.

Gallagher, Kathleen. "Bigger's Great Leap to the Figurative." *CLA Journal* 27 (1984): 293–314.

Gayle, Addison. *Richard Wright: Ordeal of a Native Son.* Garden City, N. Y.: Doubleday, 1980.

Gibson, Donald B. "Wright's Invisible Native Son." *American Quarterly* 21 (1969): 728–38.

———, ed. *Five Black Writers: Essays on Wright, Ellison, Baldwin, Hughes, and LeRoi Jones.* New York: New York University Press, 1970.

Green, Gerald. "Back to Bigger." In *Proletarian Writers of the Thirties*, edited by David Madden. Carbondale: Southern Illinois University Press, 1968.

Grenander, M. E. "Criminal Responsibility in *Native Son* and *Knock on Any Door*." *American Literature* 49 (1977): 221–33.

Gross, Barry. "Art and Act: The Example of Richard Wright." *Obsidian* 2, no. 2 (1976): 5–19.

———. " 'Intellectual Overlordship': Blacks, Jews, and *Native Son*." *Journal of Ethnic Studies* 5, no. 3 (Fall 1977): 51–59.

Gross, Seymour L. " 'Dalton' and Color-Blindness in *Native Son*." *Mississippi Quarterly: The Journal of Southern Culture* 27 (1973–74): 75–77.

Gysin, Fritz. *The Grotesque in American Negro Fiction: Jean Toomer, Richard Wright, and Ralph Ellison*. Bern, Switzerland: Francke, 1975.

Hakutani, Yoshinobu. "*Native Son* and *American Tragedy*: Two Different Interpretations of Crime and Guilt." *The Centennial Review* 23 (1978): 208–26.

———, ed. *Critical Essays on Richard Wright*. Boston: G. K. Hall, 1982.

Hoeveler, Diane Long. "Oedipus Agonistes: Mothers and Sons in Richard Wright's Fiction." *Black American Literature Forum* 12 (1978): 65–68.

Housman, John. "*Native Son* on Stage." *New Letters* 38, no. 2 (1971): 71–82.

Howe, Irving. "Black Boys and Native Sons." In *A World More Attractive*, 98–122. New York: Horizon, 1963.

Hughes, Carl M. *The Negro Novelist*. New York: Citadel, 1953.

James, Charles L. "Bigger Thomas in the Seventies: A Twentieth-Century Search for Significance." *The English Record* 22, no. 1 (Fall 1971): 6–14.

Joyce, Joyce Anne. *Richard Wright's Art of Tragedy*. Iowa City: University of Iowa Press, 1986.

———. "Style and Meaning in Richard Wright's *Native Son*." *Black American Literature Forum* 16 (1982): 112–15.

Keady, Sylvia H. "Richard Wright's Women Characters and Inequality." *Black American Literature Forum* 10 (1976): 124–28.

Kearns, Edward. "The 'Fate' Section of *Native Son*." *Contemporary Literature* 12 (1971): 146–55.

Kennedy, James G. "The Content and Form of *Native Son*." *College English* 34 (1972): 269–83.

Kent, George E. "Richard Wright: Blackness and the Adventure of Western Culture." In *Blackness and the Adventure of Western Culture*. Chicago: Third World, 1972.

Kinnamon, Keneth. *The Emergence of Richard Wright*. Urbana: University of Illinois Press, 1972.

Klotman, Phyllis R. "Moral Distancing as a Rhetorical Technique in *Native Son*: A Note on 'Fate.' " *CLA Journal* 18 (1974): 284–91.

Kostelanetz, Richard. "The Politics of Unresolved Quests in the Novels of Richard Wright." *Xavier University Studies* 8 (1969): 31–64.

Larsen, R. B. V. "The Four Voices of Richard Wright's *Native Son*." *Negro American Literature Forum* 6 (1972): 105–9.

Lee, A. Robert. "Richard Wright's Inside Narratives." In *American Fiction: New Readings*, edited by Richard Gray. London: Vision, 1983.

McCall, Dan. *The Example of Richard Wright*. New York: Harcourt, Brace & World, 1969.

Macksey, Richard, and Frank E. Moorer, eds. *Richard Wright: A Collection of Critical Essays*. Englewood Cliffs, N.J.: Prentice-Hall, 1984.

Margolies, Edward. *The Art of Richard Wright*. Carbondale: Southern Illinois University Press, 1969.

Miller, Eugene E. "Voodoo Parallels in *Native Son*." *CLA Journal* 16 (1972): 81–95.

Nagel, James. "Images of 'Vision' in *Native Son*." *The University Review* 35 (1969): 109–15.

Pudaloff, Ross. "Celebrity as Identity: Richard Wright, *Native Son*, and Mass Culture." *Studies in American Fiction* 11 (1983): 3–18.

Rao, Vimak. "The Regionalism of Richard Wright's *Native Son*." *Indian Journal of American Studies* 7, no. 1 (1977): 94–102.

Ray, David, and Robert M. Farnsworth, eds. *Richard Wright: Impressions and Perspectives*. Introduction by Charles T. Davis. Ann Arbor: University of Michigan Press, 1973.

Redden, Dorothy S. "Richard Wright and *Native Son*: Not Guilty." *Black American Literature Forum* 10 (1976): 111–16.

Redding, Saunders. "The Alien Land of Richard Wright." In *Soon One Morning*, edited by Herbert Hill, 50–59. New York: Knopf, 1965.

Reed, Kenneth T. "*Native Son*: An American *Crime and Punishment*." *Studies in Black Literature* 1, no. 2 (1970): 33–34.

Reilly, John M., ed. *Richard Wright: The Critical Reception*. New York: Franklin, 1978.

Rickels, Milton, and Patricia Rickels. *Richard Wright*. Austin: Steck-Vaughn, 1970.

Rubin, Steven J. "Richard Wright and Albert Camus: The Literature of Revolt." *International Fiction Review* 8, no. 1 (Winter 1981): 12–16.

Sadler, Jeffrey. "Split Consciousness in Richard Wright's *Native Son*." *South Carolina Review* 8, no. 2 (1976): 11–24.

Samples, Ron. "Bigger Thomas and His Descendants." *Roots* 1, no. 1 (1970): 86–93.

Savory, Jerold J. "Bigger Thomas and the Book of Job: The Epigraph of *Native Son*." *Negro American Literature Forum* 9 (1975): 55–56.

———. "Descent and Baptism in *Native Son*, *Invisible Man*, and *Dutchman*." *Christian Scholar's Review* 3 (1973): 33–37.

Scruggs, Charles W. "The Importance of the City in *Native Son*." *Ariel: A Review of International Fiction* 9, no. 3 (1978): 37–47.

Siegel, Paul N. "The Conclusion of Richard Wright's *Native Son*." *PLMA* 89 (1974): 517–23.

Singh, Ameritjit. "Misdirected Responses to Bigger Thomas." *Studies in Black Literature* 5, no. 2 (1974): 5–8.

Sisney, Mary F. "The Power and Horror of Whiteness: Wright and Ellison Respond to Poe." *CLA Journal* 29 (1985): 82–90.

Stephens, Martha. "Richard Wright's Fiction: A Reassessment." *The Georgia Review* 25 (1971): 450–70.

Stepto, Robert B. "I Thought I Knew These People: Richard Wright and the Afro-American Literary Tradition." In *Chant of Saints*, edited by Michael S. Harper and Robert B. Stepto. Urbana: University of Illinois Press, 1979.

Stern, Frederick C. "*Native Son* as Play: A Reconsideration Based on a Revival." *MELUS* 8, no. 1 (Spring 1981): 55–61.

Walls, Doyle W. "The Clue Undetected in Richard Wright's *Native Son*." *American Literature* 57 (1985): 125–28.

Wasserman, Jerry. "Embracing the Negative: *Native Son* and *Invisible Man*." *Studies in American Fiction* 4 (1976): 93–104.

Watson, Edward A. "Bessie's Blues." *New Letters* 38, no. 2 (1971): 64–70.

Wertham, Frederic. "An Unconscious Determinant in *Native Son*." In *Psychoanalysis and Literature*, edited by Hendrik M. Ruitenbeek. New York: E. P. Dutton, 1964.

Williams, John A. *The Most Native of Sons*. Garden City, N.Y.: Doubleday, 1970.

Witt, Mary Anne. "Rage and Racism in *The Stranger* and *Native Son*." *The Comparatist* 1 (1977): 35–47.

Acknowledgments

"The Bad Nigger" by Dan McCall from *The Example of Richard Wright* by Dan McCall, © 1969 by Dan McCall. Reprinted by permission of Harcourt Brace Jovanovich, Inc.

"Bigger's Infernal Assumption" (originally entitled "Lord of the Rings: *Native Son*") by Roger Rosenblatt from *Black Fiction* by Roger Rosenblatt, © 1974 by the President and Fellows of Harvard College. Reprinted by permission of Harvard University Press.

" 'What Had Made Him and What He Meant': The Politics of Wholeness in 'How "Bigger" was Born' " by Joel Roache from *Sub-Stance* 15 (1976), © 1976 by the Board of Regents of the University of Wisconsin System. Reprinted by permission of the University of Wisconsin Press.

"The Beginnings of Self-Realization" (originally entitled "Solitude: The Beginnings of Self-Realization in Zora Neale Hurston, Richard Wright, and Ralph Ellison") by Michael G. Cooke from *Afro-American Literature in the Twentieth Century* by Michael G. Cooke, © 1984 by Michael G. Cooke. Reprinted by permission.

"The Tragic Hero" (originally entitled "Characterization and Point of View: The Tragic Hero") by Joyce Anne Joyce from *Richard Wright's Art of Tragedy* by Joyce Anne Joyce, © 1986 by the University of Iowa Press. Reprinted by permission.

"The Dissociated Sensibility of Bigger Thomas" (originally entitled "The Dissociated Sensibility of Bigger Thomas in Wright's *Native Son*") by Louis Tremaine from *Studies in American Fiction* 14, no. 1 (Spring 1986), © 1986 by Northeastern University. Reprinted by permission.

Index